Puerto Rico's Future
A Time to Decide

Significant Issues Series
Timely books presenting current CSIS research and analysis of interest to the academic, business, government, and policy communities.
Managing Editor: Roberta Howard Fauriol

The Center for Strategic and International Studies (CSIS) seeks to advance global security and prosperity in an era of economic and political transformation by providing strategic insights and practical policy solutions to decisionmakers. CSIS serves as a strategic planning partner for the government by conducting research and analysis and developing policy initiatives that look into the future and anticipate change. Our more than 25 programs are organized around three themes:

Defense and Security Policy—With one of the most comprehensive programs on U.S. defense policy and international security, CSIS proposes reforms to U.S. defense organization, defense policy, and the defense industrial and technology base. Other CSIS programs offer solutions to the challenges of proliferation, transnational terrorism, homeland security, and post-conflict reconstruction.

Global Challenges—With programs on demographics and population, energy security, global health, technology, and the international financial and economic system, CSIS addresses the new drivers of risk and opportunity on the world stage.

Regional Transformation—CSIS is the only institution of its kind with resident experts studying the transformation of all of the world's major geographic regions. CSIS specialists seek to anticipate changes in key countries and regions—from Africa to Asia, from Europe to Latin America, and from the Middle East to North America.

Founded in 1962 by David M. Abshire and Admiral Arleigh Burke, CSIS is a bipartisan, nonprofit organization headquartered in Washington, D.C., with more than 220 full-time staff and a large network of affiliated experts. Former U.S. senator Sam Nunn became chairman of the CSIS Board of Trustees in 1999, and John J. Hamre has led CSIS as its president and chief executive officer since 2000.

The CSIS Press
Center for Strategic and International Studies
1800 K Street, N.W., Washington, D.C. 20006
Tel: (202) 775-3119 Fax: (202) 775-3199
E-mail: books@csis.org Web: www.csis.org

Puerto Rico's Future
A Time to Decide

DICK THORNBURGH

Foreword by George H.W. Bush

THE CSIS PRESS

Center for Strategic
and International Studies
Washington, D.C.

Significant Issues Series, Volume 29, Number 1

Printed on recycled paper in the United States of America
Cover design by Robert L. Wiser, Silver Spring, Md.
Cover photograph: Colorful buildings along San Juan Street
© Onne van der Wal/Corbis

11 10 09 08 07   5 4 3 2 1

ISSN 0736-7136
ISBN 978-0-89206-494-6

Library of Congress Cataloging-in-publication Data
Thornburgh, Dick.
Puerto Rico's future : a time to decide / Dick Thornburgh.
p. cm. — (Significant issues series ; vol. 29, no. 1)
Includes bibliographical references and index.
ISBN 978-0-89206-494-6 (pbk. : alk. paper) 1. Constitutional law—Puerto Rico. 2. Constitutional law—United States—Territories and possessions. 3. Puerto Rico—Politics and government—1952– 4. Puerto Rico—International status. 5. Puerto Rico—Relations—United States. 6. United States—Relations—Puerto Rico. 7. Statehood (American politics) 8. Self-determination, National—Puerto Rico. I. Title. II. Series.
KGV2926.T48 2007
341.26—dc22   2006101728

CONTENTS

FOREWORD

Although it has been under the American flag since 1898, very few of us know much about Puerto Rico. If fortunate enough to visit the island on one of the many cruise ships that regularly steam into the beautiful harbor of San Juan, tourists may spend a pleasant few hours strolling around and shopping in the historic Old City. Then they may reboard their liners for an overnight transit to another island without realizing that they had been just as firmly on U.S. soil as they'd been back in Port Everglades.

Today, no less than 50 years ago when West Side Story premiered on Broadway, the Stephen Sondheim lyric from that show still rings true:

Nobody knows in America
Puerto Rico's in America.

I was aware that Puerto Rico was part of the United States—but rather vague about much else—until I started campaigning in the first-ever Puerto Rican presidential primary in 1979–1980. The late, highly distinguished Puerto Rican statesman Don Luis Ferré honored me with his support and began my education in the island's complex politics. It was also Don Luis (governor of Puerto Rico from 1969 to 1973) who converted me to the cause of Puerto Rican statehood. Though scarcely a vote-getter on the mainland and hotly controversial on the island, statehood has always struck me as the right and logical destination for Puerto Rico. I favored it as president and continue to support it today.

Far from being a Caribbean micro-state, Puerto Rico contains 4 million U.S. citizens; there is an equal number on the mainland. If Puerto Rico actually were a state of the union, it would rank twenty-sixth in population, right between Kentucky and Oregon, and qualify for five or six congressional seats. Its hard-working, creative, and patriotic people have contributed much to the United States and to the Hispanic world as well. In particular, Puerto Ricans have fought bravely in all of America's wars in the twentieth and twenty-first centuries.

This patriotic service and sacrifice of Americans from Puerto Rico touched me all the more deeply for the very fact they have served with such devotion even while denied a vote for the president and members of Congress who determine when, where, and how they are asked to defend our freedoms. Only statehood can give them this. The chief problem with the current political structure of Puerto Rico—called *Estado Libre Asociado* (Free Associated State) in Spanish and "commonwealth" in English—is that it is impermanent. In 1952, Congress chose this odd-duck form of government, halfway between statehood and independence, in lieu of making Puerto Rico an "incorporated territory," which Alaska and Hawaii were at the time.

As my talented former attorney general, Dick Thornburgh, clearly demonstrates in this book, status as a territory was never intended to be permanent, either historically or constitutionally. It was a temporary transitional condition leading to statehood. So Puerto Rico's lesser status as a "commonwealth," not even an incorporated territory, is even more temporary and conditional, without being a transition to anything. The fact that Puerto Rico has managed to get along under this awkward, impermanent condition for over half a century is no justification to continue *Estado Libre Asociado.*

Recognizing the essential American democratic values at issue in this question, Dick Thornburgh's admirable work emphasizes the need for Puerto Ricans to determine their own fully permanent democratic status. This must be approved by the Congress, which the Constitution vests with full power "to dispose of and make all needful rules and regulations respecting the territory and other property belonging to the United States." But the will to change must arise from the people of Puerto Rico themselves.

That is why in my first State of the Union Address as president in 1989, I said: "I've long believed that the people of Puerto Rico should have the right to determine their own political future. Personally, I strongly favor statehood. But I urge the Congress to take the necessary steps to allow the people to decide in a referendum."

Dick Thornburgh brought his formidable intellectual powers and political skills to this issue as attorney general, more recently joining distinguished legal scholars from diverse perspectives on the status issue who offered their views to the President's Task Force on Puerto Rico's Status in 2005, and out of that experience comes this bold and compelling book. While it is not my purpose here to evaluate or give an endorsement to every proposal within it, I do applaud the author's sincere efforts to resolve this lingering constitutional conundrum. He believes, as do I, that we owe this to the Puerto Rican people and to ourselves as the world's exemplar of democracy and equal rights.

George Bush
Forty-first President of the United States

ACKNOWLEDGMENTS

I am grateful to Howard L. Hills, one of the nation's leading authorities on territorial law and policy, for his contributions to this volume. Over a period of 30 years, Mr. Hills has served as a legal adviser on territorial affairs for the National Security Council, U.S. Department of State, U.S. Department of Defense and in the U.S. Peace Corps. Mr. Hills was lead counsel for the United States in connection with the ratification and implementation of free association treaties that ended the United Nations trust territory status of Palau, the Marshall Islands and the Federated States of Micronesia. Mr. Hills has published many legal articles and policy papers on territorial status issues cited in congressional committee reports and federal court cases, including two law review articles: Howard L. Hills, *Compact of Free Association for Micronesia: Constitutional and International Law Issues,* 18 Int'l Law. 583 (1984), and Howard L. Hills, *Free Association for Micronesia and the Marshall Islands: A Transitional Political Status Model*, 27 Hawaii L. Rev. 1 (2004).

I also wish to express appreciation to my colleagues at Kirkpatrick & Lockhart Preston Gates Ellis LLP, including Glenn R. Reichardt, Shanda N. Hastings, and Philip R. Geiger, for their research, editorial, and production assistance, and to the staff of the CSIS Press, including its director James R. Dunton and its managing editor Donna Spitler Fields, for their help in preparing this work for publication.

D.T.

INTRODUCTION

This book examines the historical and constitutional framework for addressing issues related to the political status of Puerto Rico and other U.S. territories. Residents of these territories enjoy many of the rights, privileges, and benefits of U.S. citizenship under federal statutory policies, but lack permanent status or fully democratic self-government. They are deprived of basic rights of self-determination that U.S. citizens generally enjoy—rights that the United States is committed to achieving for peoples around the world. Indeed, as a party to various international agreements, covenants, and treaties, the United States has committed itself to the goals of decolonization and universal suffrage and to important human rights, including the rights of self-determination and self-government. Yet the residents of Puerto Rico and other U.S. territories, cut off from the full benefits of citizenship and the right to full self-government as separate sovereign nations, remain in a political limbo that falls far short of these goals. More important, without affirmative action by the U.S. Congress, no mechanisms are available to them under current federal law for achieving full self-government.

OVERVIEW OF THE ISSUES

For more than a century, Congress has been unwilling or unable to face and resolve the question of Puerto Rico's ultimate political status, which has also created ambiguity about the status of other smaller U.S. territories. Instead, Congress has exercised U.S. sovereignty over these territories while, at the same time, allowing territorial leaders varying degrees of control over their local affairs and territorial residents limited benefits as U.S. nationals or as "statutory" U.S. citizens. The territories and their residents have virtually no ability to influence national policy. For instance, residents of the territories cannot vote in U.S. presidential elections nor can they elect voting members of the U.S. Congress, even though Congress determines their legal rights and responsibilities and has the power to determine their ultimate political status.

In these regards, the treatment of Puerto Rico and other U.S. territories stands in sharp contrast to the way in which the United States incorporated territories into the Union under the principles of the Northwest Ordinance, the template for territorial status resolution that the very first U.S. Congress adopted in 1789. The Northwest Ordinance assumed that territorial status was a temporary step on the path toward statehood and full citizenship. Unfortunately, a confluence of poorly reasoned Supreme Court decisions and paralyzing congressional indecision, in the face of dilemmas associated with America's changing role in the world, resulted in departures from the Northwest Ordinance model. This occurred after the United States acquired several territories (including Puerto Rico) as a result of the Treaty of Peace that ended the Spanish-American War in 1898.

As this book describes, Supreme Court decisions on the status of these new territories, including the so-called *Insular Cases* of 1901, spawned the "unincorporated" territory doctrine and two decades later the Supreme Court's 1922 decision in *Balzac v. Porto Rico*, 258 U.S. 298 (1922). These rulings have led Congress and the courts to believe—incorrectly in this author's view—that conferral of U.S. citizenship on residents of Puerto Rico in 1917 left the territory and its residents with no greater rights and in the same legal and political status as unincorporated territories with noncitizen populations. The *Insular Cases*, as applied to Puerto Rico by *Balzac* after U.S. citizenship was conferred, improperly invaded the constitutional power and responsibility of Congress to determine the political status of U.S. territories whose residents were granted American citizenship. The flawed policies established under *Balzac* for Puerto Rico were then extended to other small territories that, as a practical matter, may or may not have the same political status options as Puerto Rico. Although the Supreme Court's opinion in *Balzac* recognized that the U.S. government has a constitutional obligation to respect the "fundamental rights" of people over whom it exercises sovereignty, for several decades Congress, the Supreme Court, and the executive branch have interpreted *Balzac* to mean that the U.S. Constitution does not extend to or protect certain fundamental rights of U.S. citizens in Puerto Rico and other "unincorporated" territories, including government by consent of the governed. Instead, U.S. citizens in these territories have only those rights given to them by Congress on an ad hoc, discretionary, and temporary basis.

As a result, nine decades after U.S. citizenship was granted, Puerto Rico remains the only large, populous territory under U.S. control that has never been put on the path toward either statehood or independence, despite a U.S. treaty commitment that Congress would determine the "civil rights and political status" of the residents of Puerto Rico.[1] Instead, the residents of Puerto Rico have a constitutional status akin to other historically disenfranchised classes of people who were the subjects of institutionalized discrimination and who lack meaningful access to any constitutional or political mechanism to initiate, advance, or secure a change in the U.S. law or policy that defines their less-than-equal status. Just as the Supreme Court's *Dred Scott* decision of 1857 institutionalized the subordinate status of those subject to slavery laws as persons who were less than citizens, the *Balzac* decision of 1922 institutionalized, in Puerto Rico, indefinite discrimination against the largest class of disenfranchised people that now exists under the U.S. flag. It took the Civil War and the constitutional amendments that followed to correct the inequities of the *Dred Scott* decision and other legal manifestations of disenfranchisement. More than eight decades after the *Balzac* decision, the residents of Puerto Rico still have a less-than-equal status as U.S. citizens and lack any political or legal mechanism under federal law to secure a change in their status.

Unfortunately, federal courts have been unwilling to untangle the mess created by the Supreme Court in *Balzac*, contending (paradoxically and belatedly, given the political dimensions of that 1922 ruling) that the status of Puerto Rico and its residents raises "political questions" that only Congress can resolve. In fact, as recently as 2005, a majority of the judges on the U.S. Court of Appeals for the First Circuit (the highest federal court, other than the Supreme Court, with jurisdiction over Puerto Rico) relied upon the "political question" doctrine when it declined to consider the merits of a lawsuit demanding that residents of Puerto Rico be given the right to vote for president.[2] Two judges of the First Circuit issued strongly worded dissents from the majority's opinion—arguing that, if Congress was unwilling or unable to do so, U.S. courts needed to vindicate the civil rights of the nearly 4 million U.S. citizens residing in Puerto Rico and thereby ensure that the United States honored international commitments to human rights and self-determination made in undertakings such as the International Covenant on Civil and Political Rights. But dissenting opinions do not carry the day—at least for now leaving it to Congress to reconcile the status of Puerto Rico with historical and constitutional norms for administration of U.S. territories.

The pressure on Congress ratcheted up late last year when the White House released the long-awaited and broadly welcomed "Report by the President's Task Force on Puerto Rico's Status." This document urged Congress to take steps toward the resolution of Puerto Rico's political status by sponsoring a series of referenda in Puerto Rico that would allow voters to express a preference—whether Puerto Rico should continue as a territory under federal law or seek a new nonterritory status. Only if a majority voted to end territory status would there be a vote between the nonterritory status options recognized by Congress. The White House report identifies statehood and independence as the nonterritorial options historically and currently recognized under federal law. The President's Task Force report crystallized the important choices facing Congress and the residents of Puerto Rico, calling for determination of the political status of the last large and populous U.S. territory consistent with the principle of government by consent of the governed. The response of Congress to the task force's recommendations will also have implications for the relationship between the United States and its other remaining territories.

The historical and legal analysis of federal territorial law and policy is set forth here to inform the public and Congress of the importance of these issues to the national interest and to promote a productive civic discourse about the past, present, and future of U.S. territorial administration.

THE IMPORTANCE OF RESOLVING THE POLITICAL STATUS OF PUERTO RICO

Although the residents of Puerto Rico adopted a local constitution in 1952, whereby Puerto Rico designated itself a "commonwealth," and although persons born in Puerto Rico have been granted U.S. citizenship by federal statute, Puerto Rico's legal and constitutional status has not changed: it remains an unincorporated territory of the United States, subject to the control of Congress, with a form of limited self-government, defined by federal statutory policy, concerning local matters not otherwise governed or limited by federal law.[3] Although residents of Puerto Rico have a form of U.S. citizenship that includes certain "fundamental rights," such as due process of law, and many privileges of citizenship, such as the right to travel with U.S. passports, they have no right to vote in national elections, and their sole representative in the U.S. Congress is a nonvoting emissary to the U.S. House of Representatives. As a result, they cannot participate in developing U.S. law or foreign policy, nor do they have any vote in the legislative body that controls their destiny through laws and governmental policies.

The disenfranchisement of the people of Puerto Rico for more than a century, since the United States acquired Puerto Rico from Spain at the end of the nineteenth century, cannot be squared with our nation's historic commitments to equality and self-determination, with the international treaties and covenants the United States has joined since World War II, or with other steps the United States has taken during the past 50 years to resolve the political status of territories under U.S. control—e.g., the admission of Alaska and Hawaii as states of the Union and termination of the U.S.-administered United Nations trusteeship over Micronesia and other Pacific island territories. Although other U.S. territories suffer similar disadvantages, Puerto Rico's status as the largest, most populous, and most economically significant creates special reasons why the United States should now address the steps necessary to ensure self-determination and full self-governance for U.S. citizens there.

Puerto Rico is currently home to nearly 4 million U.S. citizens—a population equal to or greater than that of 25 U.S. states. Furthermore, as statutory U.S. citizens, persons born in Puerto Rico have been allowed by Congress to migrate, without restriction, to the mainland of the United States. Approximately 4 million persons of Puerto Rican birth or descent currently reside within the United States, many of them with strong ties to family on the island and an intense interest in the relationship of Puerto Rico to the United States. For these and other reasons, the people of Puerto Rico represent a culturally and socially significant part of American society.

Puerto Rico depends financially on U.S. support, and thus the United States has a vital interest in its economic health. The federal subsidy of

Puerto Rico's "commonwealth" system of limited internal self-government is currently estimated at $16 billion annually and is growing each year.[4]

Puerto Rico holds strategic importance as the U.S. military's southeastern-most stronghold, for more than a century housing one of the largest U.S. military bases in the world at Roosevelt Roads. Although the major bases in Puerto Rico have been closed, operations could be reactivated if needed in the future, and Puerto Rico continues as an important area for U.S. military recruitment, ranking alongside the top five U.S. states in per capita military service. Given the size of Puerto Rico's population, its economic and strategic importance to the United States, and the changes taking place in Latin America and the Caribbean, the territorial model for U.S. administration of Puerto Rico—under which millions of people remain disenfranchised and without an equal voice at the national level—has become even more of an anachronism.

Past efforts to move Puerto Rico toward a permanent status—as a state or as an independent nation—have foundered, because of lack of interest in and guidance by Congress and because of the resulting confusion among residents of Puerto Rico. Plebiscites to consider status options that were held in 1967, 1993, and 1998 have been ineffective and inconclusive.[5] The President's Task Force report has proposed a series of steps that Congress and the people of Puerto Rico can take to resolve the political status of Puerto Rico and set it on the path toward a permanent status.

ORGANIZATION OF THIS BOOK

Chapter 1 describes the treatment of U.S. territories since the first Congress adopted the Northwest Ordinance. Chapter 2 outlines the constitutional framework for the consideration of territorial issues and summarizes the most significant opinions of the Supreme Court on territorial issues, particularly as they pertain to Puerto Rico. Chapter 3 discusses the international law context of these territorial issues. Chapter 4 describes recent efforts by the executive branch to clarify the status of Puerto Rico and other territories. Chapter 5 discusses the problems with so-called enhanced commonwealth proposals that have been made by the pro-commonwealth party in Puerto Rico. Finally, chapter 6 describes possible avenues to solutions—through Congress and, if necessary, the courts.

Notes

[1] "Treaty of Peace between the United States of America and the Kingdom of Spain," April 11, 1899, *United States Statutes at Large* 30:1754, art. IX.

[2] *Igartúa de la Rosa v. United States*, 417 F.3d 145 (1st Cir. 2005).

[3] *Harris v. Rosario*, 446 U.S. 651 (1980); *Rodriguez v. Popular Democratic Party*, 457 U.S. 1 (1982).

[4] Carlos Márquez, "Independence: Could Puerto Rico Go It Alone?" *Caribbean Business* 34, no. 2 (January 19, 2006): 19. See generally Alexander Odishelidze and Arthur Laffer, *Pay to the Order of Puerto Rico: The Cost of Dependence to the American Taxpayer* (Fairfax, Va.: Allegiance Press, 2004), which suggests that it costs the United States $22 billion annually to maintain Puerto Rico as a territory.

[5] However, see *The Results of the 1998 Puerto Rico Plebiscite*, regarding the most recent local status vote of December 13, 1998, in which no status option received a majority. "Statehood" received the highest vote of any status option (46.5 percent), "commonwealth" (defined as territorial by federal law) received 0.01 percent of the vote, and "none of the above" received 50.2 percent, arguably withdrawing consent of voters to continued territorial status, but not defining what nonterritorial status voters prefer. U.S. House Committee on Resources, *The Results of the 1998 Puerto Rico Plebiscite*, prepared by Chairman Don Young and senior democratic member George Miller, 106th Cong., 1st sess., 1999, Committee Print, Appendix D.

CHAPTER ONE

HISTORY OF THE TREATMENT OF U.S. TERRITORIES

NORTHWEST ORDINANCE MODEL FOR INCORPORATION LEADING TO STATEHOOD

Between 1796 and 1959, 32 territories administered under U.S. federal sovereign powers were admitted as states of the Union.[1] This historic expansion of the political order and geographic realm of the United States was accomplished under the model for territorial *incorporation* originally embodied in the Northwest Ordinance of 1787.[2]

The Continental Congress adopted the Northwest Ordinance to govern territories in the Ohio Valley that had been claimed by the United States.[3] In one of its earliest legislative acts, the first U.S. Congress adopted the Northwest Ordinance, in amended form, as the territorial policy of the United States.[4] Thus, from the very beginning of the United States, territorial incorporation—i.e., the process whereby territories were put on a path toward incorporation into the federal Union as states—was the normative federal statutory policy for governing and resolving the political status of territories the United States acquired by sovereign claim, conquest, or purchase.[5] During the continental expansion westward, this territorial incorporation policy led, without exception, to constitutional processes whereby every territory was ultimately admitted as a state.[6] The Northwest Ordinance model for incorporation of territories into states did not run its course across the North American continent until 1912, when New Mexico and Arizona became states.[7]

DEPARTURES FROM THE INCORPORATION MODEL: AMERICA FACES THE DILEMMAS OF IMPERIALISM

Outside the contiguous states and territories of the North American continent, the Northwest Ordinance model for territorial incorporation proved not to be adaptable enough to govern unprecedented territorial policy problems that arose near the end of the nineteenth century, particularly as the United States faced dilemmas associated with its new role as an emerging world power with the interests of an empire in the Western Hemisphere and elsewhere. Congress and the courts were sharply divided over America's role in the world and how the United States should treat new island territories acquired through war or international negotiation. Rather than put all these territories on the path toward statehood, some (Cuba and the Philippines) were readied for independence, others (like American Samoa) were explicitly designated and openly treated as colonies to be administered by the federal government, and yet others (such as Puerto Rico and Guam) were defined as "unincorporated territories" and allowed various degrees of local autonomy, but remained subject to the supremacy of federal law, without a clear policy about how to resolve the issue of a future political status. Only two noncontiguous territories administered by the United States after 1900—Alaska and Hawaii—were subsequently admitted to statehood.[8]

Federal territorial policies and practices deviating from the Northwest Ordinance model for territorial incorporation began in earnest after the end of the Spanish-American War, when, under the Treaty of Peace signed with Spain on December 10, 1898, the United States acquired sovereignty or control over Cuba, Guam, the Philippines, and Puerto Rico.[9] By 1900 the United States also had acquired other remote island territories, referred to as "insular" areas, some of which were inhabited and some of which were not. The smaller of these territories were less likely candidates for incorporation into states than the large territories acquired from Spain, thus ushering in the problem of long-term governance of nonstate areas. Indefinite territory status for an uninhabited territory, or even a small unincorporated territory with a noncitizen population, represents one set of policy and legal issues, but indefinite federal governance of a large territory with a U.S. citizen population poses a different and profoundly complicated set of national policy and constitutional issues.

U.S. policy toward the island territories acquired in 1898 and thereafter has varied, depending in large measure upon the size and location of each territory, its local politics and economic significance, and changing attitudes within Congress and the executive branch. Eleven small island territories with little or no population or local government (like Bajo Nuevo in the Caribbean Sea and Midway Atoll in the Pacific Ocean) have been treated as "unorganized" territories under U.S. control.[10] Cuba and the Philippines were put on a path toward independence. But U.S. policy toward its five remaining island territories (American Samoa, Guam, Puerto Rico, the Northern Mariana Islands, and the U.S. Virgin Islands) has been marked by inconsistency and indecision.

Unlike Alaska and Hawaii, none of these territories has yet been recognized under federal law and policy as incorporated areas on the path to admission to the Union as states. Instead, these territories are categorized as "unincorporated territories" that are not clearly recognized as being on a path toward either statehood or independence, but remain subject to the supreme sovereignty of Congress under the Territorial Clause of the U.S. Constitution. Congress—with the approval if not the encouragement of the courts—has consigned these unincorporated territories to a political limbo that allows each territory's residents some measure of control over their local affairs, but no direct voice in U.S. policy or in the election of U.S. national leaders and no federally recognized process by which residents of those territories can consent to the continuation of their current status or change their political status in favor of either statehood or nationhood.[11]

Congress has passed "organic" laws that have enabled these "organized" territories to establish local governments and to enact local laws that are consistent with and subject to federal law.[12] These territories tend to share certain fundamental features of unincorporated territory status.[13] Each territory's local government typically administers the civil affairs of the territory that are not otherwise governed by federal law.[14] Military and international relations remain federal matters beyond local control.[15] For some organized territories, the federal organic law has established the structure of the local government and the procedures for promulgation of local law.[16] In other cases, the organic acts of Congress authorized the adoption of local constitutions.[17] In all organized territories, federal law remains supreme in all matters and local laws are null and void to the extent they are inconsistent with applicable federal law.[18]

Not surprisingly, there are also many unique features to the relationship that each of these island territories has with the United States.[19] In some territories (e.g., Guam and Puerto Rico), residents have been granted statutory U.S. citizenship, a policy of social integration.[20] On the other hand, Congress has occasionally implemented a statutory policy that suggests separateness from the rest of the nation, sometimes purporting to treat a territory the same as a foreign jurisdiction—e.g., failed experiments treating Puerto Rico as foreign for certain tax policy purposes.[21]

The remainder of this chapter describes how U.S. policy has developed and changed for each of the territories that the United States has declined to treat as "incorporated" territories since broad deviations from the Northwest Ordinance model began after 1898.

Territories Acquired from Spain in 1898

Cuba

Under the Treaty of Peace ending the Spanish-American War,[22] the Kingdom of Spain relinquished its claims over Cuba, and the United States accepted responsibility for Cuba as an occupying power.[23] In this respect, the treatment of Cuba was distinguished from the treaty's treatment of the Philippines, Puerto Rico, and Guam, as to which Spain ceded sovereignty, resulting in U.S. territorial status for these island groups.[24]

There is a certain irony that the Spanish-American War began after the USS *Maine* exploded in Havana Harbor and liberation of Cuba was the focus of the American war effort, but Cuba was the only Spanish colony to progress under U.S. administration almost immediately to independence, without being governed under the U.S. territorial law and policy that Congress applied to the Philippines, Puerto Rico, or Guam. Rather, in accordance with its treaty with Spain, the United States recognized Cuba's independence under terms that ended its occupation and turned over its responsibilities to the new Cuban national government,[25] although the United States asserted, as a matter of hemispheric policy, the right to intervene if needed to preserve Cuba's independence.[26] U.S. influence and interest in Cuba after its independence followed a course of history that is well known and outside the realm of territorial law and policy.

The Philippines

Less well known is the history of U.S. territorial administration of the Philippines under the Treaty of Peace with Spain. Under the treaty, Spain ceded sovereignty over the Philippines to the United States,[27] and the power to govern the ceded territory and to determine the "civil rights and political status of the native inhabitants" was vested in the U.S. Congress.[28] As a matter of international law, the treaty merely recognized the sovereignty of the United States, but under the U.S. Constitution and the domestic U.S. system of federalism, the treaty meant that the Philippines would be governed as a U.S. territory under the Territorial Clause.

The first order of business for the United States in the Philippines was to suppress through force of arms the insurrection against foreign rule led by pro-independence patriot Emilio Aguinaldo.[29] In 1900 a Philippines Commission was sent by President McKinley to determine when and how to inaugurate civilian government once the insurgency was put down.[30] While American forces occupying the country at the time of Spanish surrender accomplished their mission to bring an end to internal hostilities, the debate in Congress over the future status of the Philippines was resolved in favor of independence.[31] Thus, Congress rejected, in the case of the noncontiguous Philippines territory, extension of the same manifest destiny ideology that drove continental expansion of the United States under the Northwest Ordinance model of territorial incorporation. Instead, Congress approved a declaration of intent to grant independence to the Philippines.[32]

That declaration by Congress was entitled: "An Act to declare the purpose of the people of the United States as to the future political status of the people of the Philippine Islands, and to provide a more autonomous government . . . ."[33] The declaration went on to state that "it was never the intention of the people of the United States in the incipiency of the War with Spain to make it a war of conquest or for territorial aggrandizement . . . it is, as it has always been, the purpose of the people of the United States to withdraw their sovereignty over the Philippine Islands and to recognize their independence as soon as a stable government can be established . . . ."[34]

Consistent with its declared intent, under the 1916 statute Congress made federal law inapplicable to the Philippines, unless specifically and expressly made applicable.[35] The local legislature was provided with general legislative power, except that Congress could annul any local act it disapproved.[36] The governor general was appointed by the president of the United States, but U.S. policy clearly was to foster a political and legal system outside the U.S. domestic legal and political process.[37] Although people born in the territory had U.S. *nationality* at birth under federal statutory policy and continued to owe allegiance at the national level to the United States, the local legislature was authorized to confer upon them territorial *citizenship* of the Philippines.[38]

In 1934 the process of succession to independent nation-state status was advanced by the enactment of the Tydings-McDuffie Act (officially the Philippine Independence Act).[39] This was the first experiment by Congress in an overseas territory with the "commonwealth" structure of local self-government under a locally adopted constitution. Unlike later "commonwealth" models in the Northern Mariana Islands and Puerto Rico, which were forms of local civil administration of an organized but unincorporated territory for an indefinite period of time,[40] the Commonwealth of the Philippines was a form of local self-government "pending the final and complete withdrawal of the sovereignty of the United States over the Philippine Islands."[41]

In other words, the "commonwealth" structure of the local government in the Philippines was intended to become the national government of an independent Philippines. Until independence occurred, however, Section 2(a)(1) of the Tydings-McDuffie Act provided that "[a]ll citizens of the Philippine Islands shall owe allegiance to the United States," and Section 2(a)(2) required every official of the "commonwealth" government to take an oath that he or she "recognizes and accepts the supreme authority of and will maintain true faith and allegiance to the United States."

The Tydings-McDuffie Act also prescribed "house-keeping" policies, such as procedures for the transfer of U.S. property to the new national government, as part of an orderly transition to independence.[42] Although the succession to independence was interrupted by the Japanese invasion and occupation of the Philippines during World War II, as soon as practicable after the defeat of Japan and a lot sooner than millions of Filipino people desired, the United States ended its colonial experiment in the Philippines by declaring and recognizing it as an independent nation.[43]

Prior to independence, many Filipinos had taken advantage of their U.S. nationality to migrate to the U.S. mainland and to begin new lives there with permanent residence as allowed by Congress during the territorial period. Upon termination of the Philippines' territorial status and its transition to independence, all persons with U.S. national status based on birth in the Philippines became nonimmigrant aliens under U.S. immigration law, lost the permanent residence rights they had as nationals, and were repatriated to the former territory.[44] Under Section 14 of the Tydings-McDuffie Act, thousands who had become permanent residents in the United States were involuntarily detained and transported back to the Philippines.[45]

Legal challenges to this compulsory repatriation policy went to the U.S. Supreme Court, which upheld the enforcement of Section 14 of the Tydings-McDuffie Act and recognized that the Philippines had become an independent country with separate sovereignty, nationality, and citizenship.[46] Conferral as well as withdrawal of U.S. nationality status and territorial citizenship created by statute under the Territorial Clause was deemed by the Court to be within the discretion of Congress under the unincorporated territory doctrine of the *Insular Cases*, and the Supreme Court subsequently recognized the same degree of congressional discretion with respect to statutory nationality and citizenship conferred by statute enacted pursuant to the Naturalization Clause.[47]

As discussed further below, the lesson of the Philippine repatriation for residents of the remaining U.S. territories is that a congressional policy conferring statutory nationality status, as well as statutory U.S. or territorial citizenship, can be ended under the same power by which it was instituted, whether it is the Territorial Clause, the Naturalization Clause, or both. Although Fourteenth Amendment nationality and citizenship generally is beyond the reach of Congress, all forms of U.S. nationality status and citizenship acquired under federal statutory policy rather than the Fourteenth Amendment can be made subject to an election of allegiance and denied to unborn descendants by act of Congress as part of the transition to separate sovereign nationhood.[48]

Puerto Rico

The United States also acquired sovereignty over Puerto Rico and its adjacent islands under the Treaty of Peace that ended the Spanish-American War.[49] As with the Philippines, Article IX of the treaty stated with respect to Puerto Rico that "[t]he civil rights and political status of the native inhabitants of the territories hereby ceded to the United States shall be determined by the Congress."[50]

In the exercise of its authority and responsibilities under the Territorial Clause, Congress has enacted a succession of statutory policies for gradually increased local self-government in Puerto Rico.[51] But those policies have not established full self-government or the complete implementation of the principle of government by consent of the governed.[52]

The first statutory policy aimed at institution building in Puerto Rico was the Foraker Act, which Congress passed in April 1900 to establish civil administration of territorial affairs in Puerto Rico.[53] The Foraker Act also created the office of Puerto Rico's resident commissioner, a non-voting member of the U.S. House of Representatives with a four-year term, instead of the usual two-year term.[54] In 1917 Congress passed the Jones Act, which increased local authority over the administration of civil affairs in Puerto Rico and conferred U.S. citizenship on all persons born in Puerto Rico.[55]

In 1950, to promote progress toward greater local self-government, Congress approved Public Law 600,[56] which created a process for joint approval by Congress and the residents of Puerto Rico of a local constitution that would govern the administration of Puerto Rico's internal civil affairs.[57] The proposed process for joint adoption of a local constitution, in accordance with Public Law 600, was approved by the voters of Puerto Rico in an island-wide referendum on June 4, 1951.[58] On September 17, 1951, the Constitutional Convention of Puerto Rico was convened, pursuant to Public Law 600.[59] The Constitutional Convention approved the proposed constitution of the Commonwealth of Puerto Rico on February 6, 1952.[60] That proposed constitution was approved by voters in an island-wide referendum in Puerto Rico on March 2, 1952.[61]

The local constitution ratified by the voters of Puerto Rico was approved by Congress on July 3, 1952, subject to certain amendments.[62] The powers of the local government in Puerto Rico are expressly subject, under Article I, Section 1, of the constitution,[63] to conformity with federal law. The local constitution's reservation of sovereignty to the people under Article I, Section 2, relates to local matters not governed by federal law. The "compact" referred to in Article I, Section 1, of the constitution of Puerto Rico is subject to and exists only as permissively allowed at the discretion of Congress.[64] Under the Supremacy Clause (Article VI) of the U.S. Constitution and Section 734 of Title 48 of the U.S. Code, federal law nullifies incompatible local law, not vice versa.[65] Thus, the constitution of Puerto Rico does not accord to the residents of Puerto Rico any meaningful form of consent to the promulgation and application in Puerto Rico of federal law, which remains the supreme law of Puerto Rico. Furthermore, by adopting amendments to Puerto Rico's constitution to require that future changes in the local constitution conform to federal law, Congress rejected any suggestion that, as a "commonwealth,"[66] Puerto Rico had achieved a nonterritorial association with the United States that was not subject to principles of federal supremacy.[67]

The congressionally required amendments to the constitution were accepted by the Constitutional Convention of Puerto Rico on July 10, 1952.[68] On July 25, 1952, the governor of Puerto Rico, as authorized by Congress, proclaimed the constitution of Puerto Rico to be in effect.[69] On November 4, 1952, the congressionally required amendments to the constitution were ratified by the voters of Puerto Rico in a referendum conducted for that purpose.[70]

Based on the fact that the inhabitants of Puerto Rico had given their consent to a constitution that provided a "commonwealth" structure of self-government in respect of local matters not otherwise governed by federal law, the United Nations (UN) General Assembly, on November 27, 1953, adopted UN Resolution 748 (VIII), which relieved the United States from the UN requirement that it file reports on Puerto Rico as a non-self-governing area under Article 73 of the UN Charter.[71] However, Paragraph 9 of Resolution 748 expressly recognized that both the United States and Puerto Rico retain the ability to seek, through their respective constitutional processes, changes in federal-territorial relations or Puerto Rico's political status.[72]

In advance of the vote in the United Nations adopting Resolution 748, the United States circulated to the General Assembly a legal memorandum stating that the precise legal and political nature of Puerto Rico's "commonwealth" was subject to the supremacy of federal law as "interpreted by judicial decision" of U.S. courts.[73] In accordance with that legal position, federal courts have subsequently recognized that Congress still governs the Commonwealth of Puerto Rico under Article IX of the 1898 Treaty of Peace with Spain and the Territorial Clause of the U.S. Constitution.[74] The U.S. Supreme Court's rulings on the legal meaning of measures Congress has adopted to govern Puerto Rico (including the Jones Act, which conferred statutory U.S. citizenship on persons born in Puerto Rico in 1917, and Public Law 600, which authorized local constitutional government in 1950) confirm that Puerto Rico's status remains that of a territory, and the "commonwealth" system of local self-government remains subject in all matters whatsoever to the plenary authority of Congress in the exercise of its powers under the Territorial Clause.[75]

Although efforts occasionally have been made in Congress to put Puerto Rico on the path toward final resolution of its ultimate status—

i.e., as a state or an independent nation—or instead to confirm the consent of the people to remain an unincorporated territory with limited self-government under the "commonwealth" system, those efforts have been stymied thus far.[76] As a result, Puerto Rico remains a territory that has achieved constitutional self-government as a "commonwealth" only in respect of its internal affairs and civil administration, subject to the supremacy of federal law.[77] Until that status changes, the residents of Puerto Rico will not achieve the right to full self-government or the equal rights of national citizenship they would otherwise have by incorporation of Puerto Rico into the United States or through the independence of Puerto Rico as a sovereign nation.[78] Only Congress can adopt the measures required for a political resolution of Puerto Rico's final status, because no form of local government created by statute can be converted into a permanent nonterritorial form of self-government with vested political rights that confer full democratic self-government at the level of national sovereignty.[79]

U.S. presidents and individual members of Congress have frequently suggested that the federal government is ready to accept whatever political status the people of Puerto Rico might choose. But those suggestions are largely hollow because, under the Territorial Clause of the U.S. Constitution, only Congress has the power to define the alternatives for Puerto Rico's future and the terms for Puerto Rico's transition from territorial status to something other than that.[80] Any plebiscite by voters in Puerto Rico among locally formulated status alternatives that might or might not assure their transition to full self-government is inconclusive and potentially disruptive unless the alternatives presented to the voters have previously been approved by Congress and are carefully explained to Puerto Rico's electorate.

Past plebiscites that were not authorized by Congress (and, therefore, were without legal effect) demonstrate the problem. In a plebiscite on July 23, 1967, a clear majority of Puerto Rican voters (60.5 percent) favored "commonwealth" status over the alternatives of "statehood" (38.9 percent) or "independence" (0.5 percent).[81] The problem with the 1967 proposed "commonwealth" choice, however, was that it was never accepted by Congress, and "commonwealth" itself represents nothing more than a continuation of Puerto Rico's territorial status as implemented by federal statutes, which can never in itself create vested rights of full self-government.[82] Furthermore, subsequent plebiscites suggested that most residents of Puerto Rico wanted to move away from "commonwealth" status, particularly when it is defined by reference to federal law as a territorial status, but the lack of congressionally accepted status options once again produced confusing results. Thus, in a plebiscite on November 14, 1993, the "commonwealth" alternative (even when that alternative was defined by the local pro-commonwealth party) received less than a majority of all votes (48.6 percent) and only slightly more votes than the "statehood" option (46.4 percent).[83] Once again, independence for Puerto Rico was favored by only a small minority of the voters (4.5 percent).[84]

In December 1994, the Legislative Assembly of Puerto Rico reacted to the results of the 1993 plebiscite by petitioning Congress to: (a) implement the status option that had received the plurality of votes ("commonwealth" status as defined by the local pro-commonwealth party) or (b) if Congress was unwilling to do that, adopt a federal legislative policy measure that "states the specific status alternatives [Congress] is willing to consider, and the measures it recommends that the People of Puerto Rico should take as part of the process to solve the problem of their political status."[85]

Congress did not immediately respond to this petition from the Puerto Rican legislature. Approximately two years later, in January 1997, the Legislative Assembly once again petitioned Congress, this time to sponsor a political status referendum on terms leading to a nonterritorial status.[86] After four years of hearings and deliberations, the U.S. House of Representatives finally responded by passing H.R. 856—the United States–Puerto Rico Political Status Act—on March 4, 1998. H.R. 856 was the first bill passed by either house of the Congress that would have offered the residents of Puerto Rico a choice among the following defined status options: (a) statehood, (b) independence (including sovereign free association with the United States) or (c) continued status as an unincorporated territory, with a "commonwealth" model for local constitutional self-government.[87] But H.R. 856 did not become law.

The local political party that supports Puerto Rico's current "commonwealth" structure of local government successfully opposed Senate passage of a similar bill,[88] based on its party platform favoring "enhanced commonwealth" status for Puerto Rico (which was rejected in overwhelming bipartisan votes in the U.S. House of Representatives and not included as a status option under H.R. 856 as passed by the

House).[89] Instead, the Senate adopted Resolution 279, a nonbinding measure that expressed support for status resolution in equivocal and ambiguous terms that emphasized the plenary power of Congress to determine territorial status, without indicating what status options the Senate might approve.[90]

Three months later, another plebiscite was held in Puerto Rico. This plebiscite, which was also without federal authorization, added more confusion to the political status debate. Like the 1967 and 1993 locally sponsored votes, the 1998 vote was conducted under local statutory law. This time, the voters were given more choices: (a) continuation of Puerto Rico's current status, which, for purposes of this plebiscite, was defined in accordance with federal law as territorial status; (b) statehood; (c) independence; (d) "free association"; and (e) "none of the above."[91] Once Puerto Rico's current "commonwealth" was presented on a ballot as defined by federal law (i.e., as a territory), rather than in the "enhanced" form proposed by the local pro-commonwealth party, that option received less than one-tenth of 1 percent of the vote (0.01 percent).[92] The statehood option received the most votes for a status option, but still less than a majority (46.5 percent), and "none of the above" was favored by a razor thin majority of the voters (50.2 percent).[93] What that choice means has confused people in Congress and throughout the United States, including Puerto Rico.

Thus, despite various efforts in Congress and within Puerto Rico to define coherent procedures for Puerto Rico's progress toward status resolution, the end result has been inconclusive and nonbinding local status votes that have devolved into disturbingly bitter and frustrating exercises in stunningly misinformed ideological confrontation and demoralizing political futility. By failing to clarify the true nature of Puerto Rico's current territorial status and the limited rights of U.S. citizens in Puerto Rico, and by failing to sponsor a referendum process based on legally valid options, Congress has left U.S. citizens in Puerto Rico who hope for a dignified permanent status without a well-informed and valid path toward democratic self-determination.

As a result, the process of achieving full self-determination in Puerto Rico is in or near a state of arrest. This state of affairs is inconsistent with international commitments made by the United States, and is at odds with the stated policy objective of U.S. foreign policy, which is to advance democracy and self-determination for peoples throughout the world.[94] Furthermore, at least one result of the contentious and controversial local status votes in Puerto Rico over the past few decades is that it can now be argued that the voters of Puerto Rico, by virtual unanimous rejection of "commonwealth" as it is defined by federal law (i.e., territorial), have effectively withdrawn their consent to be governed under the current territorial status model.

Guam

Guam is identified in Article II and Article V of the Treaty of Peace that ended the Spanish-American War as an island that would be ceded to the United States and evacuated by Spain at the same time that Spain evacuated the Philippines.[95] The Treaty of Peace began more than a century of unincorporated territory status for Guam.

Guam was administered by the U.S. Navy for the first half of the twentieth century.[96] The residents of the territory were U.S. nationals who endured four years of brutal Japanese occupation during World War II.[97] In 1950 the Guamanians were granted statutory U.S. citizenship.[98] In that same year, Congress adopted an organic act establishing local self-government for Guam.[99] Over the years, Congress grew weary of frequent requests from the three branches of Guam's local government for amendments to the Guam Organic Act. So, in 1976, it authorized Guam to adopt a local constitution[100] giving Guam the same "commonwealth" model for internal self-government that Congress had permitted in Puerto Rico[101] and the Northern Mariana Islands.[102]

Political leaders in Guam attempted to take Congress up on its offer of greater local self-government by convening a constitutional convention in 1977 under the federal enabling law.[103] However, a proposed constitution for Guam was rejected by voters in a 1979 referendum, due in part to opposition from local leaders who wanted to address Guam's political status before adopting a territorial constitution. Based on speculation that the United States would terminate its annual reports to the United Nations under Article 73(e) of the UN Charter after adoption of a local constitution, as in the case of Puerto Rico after that island adopted its local constitution in 1953,[104] Guam's local legislature sought assurances from Congress that ratification of a Guam constitution would not become an excuse to make unincorporated territory status perpetual by denying future self-determination on other political status options.[105]

After Guam's draft constitution was defeated, Guam's "Commission on Self-Determination" submitted a new "commonwealth" proposal to the voters that included not only local constitutional government, but also enhanced features of autonomy sought but never achieved under "commonwealth" models approved by Congress for Puerto Rico and the Northern Mariana Islands.[106] In part, the expansive autonomy elements of Guam's new "commonwealth" proposal were influenced by the sovereign autonomy terms of the Compact of Free Association into which the United States had entered in 1986 with the nearby islands of Micronesia, the Marshall Islands, and Palau after the United States had terminated its administration of the UN trusteeship of those islands.[107]

Guam has a nonvoting delegate who serves a two-year term in the U.S. House of Representatives.[108] The delegate from Guam tried to get a hearing in Congress on Guam's new "commonwealth" proposal, which was introduced as the "Guam Commonwealth Act" in every session of Congress for 10 years. In 1997 the Committee on Resources of the U.S. House of Representatives finally scheduled a hearing to consider the Guam Commonwealth Act.[109]

Among other "innovative" elements, Guam's "commonwealth" proposal sought to give Guam's political leaders power over both domestic and international relations and purported to require the "mutual consent" of Guam and the United States to any application of federal law in Guam or to any change in Guam's autonomy as a "commonwealth." In 1994 the U.S. Interior Department's Special Representative for Guam requested a legal opinion and negotiating instructions from the U.S. Department of Justice with regard to Guam's "commonwealth" proposal. This request resulted in a Justice Department memorandum of law ("DOJ Memorandum") that was to play a significant role in the 1997 hearing on the Guam Commonwealth Act.[110] The DOJ Memorandum recognized that the United States had been inconsistent on the enforceability of mutual consent provisions in connection with territorial self-government, and recommended that mutual consent provisions adopted in the past (e.g., with respect to the Northern Mariana Islands) be honored as a matter of discretionary policy because they were made in good faith. However, the DOJ Memorandum clearly and unmistakably concluded, in footnote 2, that such promises of mutual consent should not be made because "there could not be an enforceable vested right in a political status," meaning that statutory measures defining political status and forms of territorial government are not legally binding on Congress and therefore cannot be enforced, leading to the following compelling assessment:

> The former views of this [Department] on the validity or efficacy of mutual consent . . . have not been consistent. . . . We therefore have carefully reexamined this issue. Our conclusion is that these clauses . . . are legally unenforceable . . . .[111]
>
> The inclusion of such provisions, therefore, in the Commonwealth Act would be misleading. Honesty and fair dealing forbid the inclusion of such illusory and deceptive provisions . . . .[112]

The Justice Department's candor and transparency after years of inconsistency on a sensitive constitutional issue is both rare and enlightening. This makes the legal conclusion in the DOJ Memorandum, that mutual consent provisions are statutory policies subject to the supremacy of federal law and the reserved power of Congress over territories, more compelling than if the Justice Department had merely defended its earlier positions on mutual consent provisions.

The Resources Committee hearing on October 29, 1997, was a classic demonstration of the maxim that one should be careful about what one asks for at any given moment. Based on the Justice Department's clarification of territorial law in the DOJ Memorandum, the deputy secretary of the interior, John Garamendi, told Congress the Clinton administration considered the Guam Commonwealth Act's requirement that both the United States and Guam give their "mutual consent" to the application of federal law in Guam to be unconstitutional and "inconsistent with United States sovereignty over Guam."[113] Similarly, Deputy Secretary Garamendi testified that "it is our considered view that the proposed mutual consent language cannot preclude a future Congress from unilaterally modifying or repealing the Guam Commonwealth Act."[114] This adverse testimony from the Clinton administration effectively killed the Guam Commonwealth Act.

After the Resources Committee hearing, the headlines in Guam read "No commonwealth" and "We have been betrayed."[115] Guam's political status process has stalled since then, although the local government is reportedly planning another referendum that would support giving Guam incorporated territory status that would ultimately lead to statehood, perhaps after Guam's consolidation with the Northern Mariana Islands.[116] Paradoxically, no local effort has yet been made to adopt a local constitution for Guam, which remains an unincorporated territory subject to the organic act Congress passed in 1950.

Two Other Territories Proceeded toward Statehood

It is historically and legally significant that at the same time the U.S. Supreme Court invented the unincorporated territory status policy for Puerto Rico and the Philippines, the Court adhered to the incorporated territory doctrine with respect to two other territories, Alaska and Hawaii. Although the Court construed the 1898 Treaty of Peace with Spain in a way that dramatically deviated from the Northwest Ordinance tradition of territorial incorporation, the Court came to very different conclusions when it interpreted the instruments by which the United States acquired sovereignty over Alaska and Hawaii, treating those two territories as incorporated and on the path toward statehood.[117]

President McKinley signed the act annexing Hawaii in 1898 and executed the declaration for the Treaty of Peace, by which the United States acquired Puerto Rico and other Spanish territories, in 1899. The Supreme Court's decisions in both the *Insular Cases* and in the cases regarding Alaska and Hawaii were handed down over a four-year period between 1901 and 1905.[118] How could the president and the Supreme Court simultaneously treat these two sets of territories so differently?

One answer seems clear: The Supreme Court justified the disparate treatment of Puerto Rico and the Philippines on one hand and Alaska and Hawaii on the other on the fact that Congress had extended citizenship rights, under the U.S. Constitution, to the residents of Alaska and Hawaii, but did not extend those same citizenship rights to the residents of Puerto Rico and the Philippines when Congress ratified the Treaty of Peace with Spain. As a consequence, Puerto Rico and the Philippines were treated as unincorporated territories inhabited by nationals but not citizens, and Alaska and Hawaii were treated as incorporated territories with U.S. citizen populations who were directly protected by the U.S. Constitution.

In the case of Alaska, the Supreme Court relied on language from the treaty of cession with Russia, which stated that the "inhabitants of the ceded territory . . . shall be admitted to the enjoyment of all the rights, advantages, and immunities of citizens of the United States . . . ."[119] This conferral of citizenship was not accompanied by an express statement of incorporation, and citizenship was not extended to the "uncivilized tribes" of native people until 1915, but the citizenship language in Article 3 of the treaty of cession was the primary criterion relied upon by the U.S. Supreme Court in ruling that Alaska was an incorporated territory.[120]

In the case of Hawaii, the Supreme Court ruled that the islands were incorporated in 1900 when Congress adopted an organic act[121] providing that all persons who had been citizens of Hawaii at the time of annexation were "citizens" of the United States.[122] The Supreme Court's ruling on Hawaii's status also relied upon the fact that, in the 1900 organic act, "the Constitution was formally extended to these islands."[123]

Thus, the clear import of the Supreme Court's decisions as to Alaska and Hawaii was that U.S. citizenship triggers incorporation, including extension of the U.S. Constitution to the full extent possible prior to statehood. As a result, the Court did not apply the unincorporated territory doctrine of the *Insular Cases* to these territories with U.S. citizen populations.

Although this distinction in political status may have had some logical and legal basis in the early years of the twentieth century, as discussed in chapter 2, that rationale should have been reexamined and a different result should have been obtained beginning in 1917, when Congress extended citizenship to residents of Puerto Rico.[124]

Other Island Territories Acquired through Negotiation or Purchase

American Samoa

The United States acquired sovereignty over Eastern Samoa, now known as American Samoa, after Germany and Britain renounced their claims to Samoa under the Treaty of Berlin in 1899, clearing the way for the United States to conclude treaties of cession with the chiefs of Tutuila, Manua, and Samoa, who ceded their island realms to the United States under treaties ratified by Congress in 1900 and 1904.[125]

More than any other unincorporated territory, American Samoa has been and still is governed under federal statutory policy in the classic colonial manner. All powers of government are vested by Congress in the president of the United States.[126] The territory was administered by the U.S. Navy until 1951, at which time authority was transferred to the U.S. Department of the Interior.[127]

A local government was not constituted in American Samoa for almost three decades until one was finally organized under an order of the U.S. Secretary of the Interior.[128] There is no federal organic act that establishes a local government structure in American Samoa. Instead, a local constitution approved by the U.S. interior secretary continues to provide the framework for promulgation of local law. That administratively created local constitution can be amended only by Congress.[129]

American Samoa has no federal court, and rulings from the local courts go directly to the federal courts in Hawaii. American Samoa sends a nonvoting delegate to Congress,[130] and residents of the territory have no vote in national elections. Statutory nationality has been conferred by Congress, but no separate categories of statutory U.S. citizenship were established.[131] U.S. law is supreme.[132]

American Samoa's local government has not sought increased self-government or any further resolution of its political status.[133] Being administered by the Secretary of the Interior as directed by Congress appears to suit the Samoans, especially since it preserves the traditional communal land ownership system and other local customs.[134] Although the existing political system does not advance government by consent in American Samoa, it does preserve the "Samoan way of life."[135]

The Virgin Islands

Beginning in 1867, the United States negotiated with Denmark over the possible purchase of the Virgin Islands and finally sealed the deal nearly five decades later under a treaty of cession that was signed in 1916.[136] The 1917 law approving the purchase of the Virgin Islands authorized the president to appoint a governor who would exercise "all military, civil, and judicial powers necessary to govern the West Indian Islands acquired from Denmark."[137]

For the next 14 years, U.S. Navy administrators appointed by the president exercised those powers by administering the affairs of the Virgin Islands. There had been some debate within the War Department and the U.S. State Department in Washington regarding whether the treaty with Denmark had conferred U.S. citizenship on residents of the Virgin Islands.[138] The prevailing view was that residents only had nationality under U.S. sovereignty, so in 1927 Congress conferred statutory U.S. citizenship on the Virgin Island residents.[139]

In 1931 administration of the Virgin Islands was transferred from the U.S. Navy to the U.S. Department of the Interior, which appointed a civilian governor.[140] In 1936 Congress passed a new organic act that increased local self-government within the Virgin Islands by increments.[141] Local self-government was increased to a level comparable to Guam under the Revised Organic Act of the Virgin Islands that Congress passed in 1954.[142] Under its provisions, a territorial legislature replaced the two earlier municipal councils in St. Croix and St. Thomas.[143] The Revised Organic Act also declared the Virgin Islands an unincorporated territory of the United States,[144] but the U.S. Senate Committee Report that accompanied the Act made clear that Congress had no future status policy for the Virgin Islands: "Enactment of this bill would in no way be a commitment for or step toward any status other than that set forth; namely, that of an unincorporated American territory."[145]

In 1968 the Revised Organic Act was amended to provide for an elected governor of the Virgin Islands.[146] In 1972 Congress allowed the Virgin Islands to send a nonvoting delegate to the U.S. House of Representatives with a two-year term.[147] In 1976 Congress authorized the Virgin Islands to adopt the same level of self-government as in Puerto Rico and the Northern Mariana Islands by adopting a local constitution.[148] Congress even went so far as to approve a draft constitution to be submitted to voters in the Virgin Islands, but it has not yet been ratified by voters there.[149] As a result, the Virgin Islands remain an unincorporated territory that is governed by local officials subject to the Revised Organic Act passed by Congress in 1954 and amended in 1968.

Pacific Island Trust Territories That Became Independent Nations

The United States liberated several Pacific islands from Japan in some of the bloodiest fighting during World War II. However, instead of exercising U.S. national sovereignty over these islands—which included Micronesia, the Marshall Islands, the Northern Mariana Islands, and Palau—the United States, through a 1947 agreement with the UN Security Council, acted as an Administering Authority for these island territories under the UN trusteeship system. The Trust Territory of the Pacific Islands was one of 11 UN trust territories established pursuant to Chapter XII of the UN Charter.[150] The United States continued to administer this trust territory until 1986.

Article 3 of the Trusteeship Agreement provided the following:

> The administering authority shall have full powers of administration, legislation, and jurisdiction over the territory subject to the provisions of this agreement, and may apply to the trust territory, subject to any modifications which the administering authority may consider desirable, such of the laws of the United States as it may deem appropriate to local conditions and requirements.

The United States exercised these plenary powers as UN trustee in a manner that was similar to the way the United States has exercised its plenary powers under the Territorial Clause of the U.S. Constitution with respect to unincorporated territories. For example, upon entry of the Trusteeship Agreement into force, the president of the United States ordered the U.S. Navy to disestablish the government of military occupation and to establish civil government consistent with the trusteeship.[151] This order was followed by presidential action transferring the administration of the trusteeship islands to the U.S. Department of the Interior, the same agency responsible for the small unincorporated territories that were not administered by the Executive Office of the President.[152] Article 9 of the Trusteeship Agreement also provided that "[t]he administering authority [i.e., the United States] shall be entitled to constitute the trust territory into . . . [an] administrative union . . . with other territories under United States jurisdiction . . . ."[153]

There were, however, important differences between the status of the Trust Territory islands and the unincorporated territories subject to U.S. control. For example, Article 11 of the Trusteeship Agreement provided that "[t]he administering authority shall take the necessary steps to provide the status of citizenship of the trust territory" for its inhabitants.[154] This meant that the Pacific Trust islanders remained aliens under U.S. immigration and naturalization law.

Beginning in the late 1960s and the early 1970s, sovereignty movements swept through the Pacific Island Trust Territories other than the Northern Mariana Islands. Micronesia, Palau, and the Marshall Islands organized local constitutions that were authorized by the U.S. Interior Secretary in 1979.[155] The constitutional governments of Micronesia, Palau, and the Marshall Islands then negotiated a Compact of Free Association with the United States in 1985[156] and became sovereign nations upon U.S. termination of the UN trusteeship.[157] The United States has continued to have close political ties to these Pacific islands and has provided them with substantial economic assistance even after they became independent nations.[158]

The Northern Mariana Islands: A Trust Territory That Became an Unincorporated Territory Subject to U.S. Control

Unlike the other former Pacific Island Trust Territories, the Northern Mariana Islands rejected any movement toward separate sovereignty and instead sought a closer association with the United States in the hope that it might result in U.S. citizenship for island residents. In contrast to the leaders of Micronesia, the Marshall Islands, and Palau, the elected representatives of the trust territory citizens in the Northern Mariana Islands proposed and negotiated an unprecedented agreement under which the United States acquired sovereignty over their islands. This agreement, known as the "Covenant to Establish a Commonwealth of the Northern Mariana Islands (CNMI) in Political Union with the United States of America," was approved by the voters of the Northern Mariana Islands in a UN-observed plebiscite in 1975 and then ratified by the U.S. Congress in 1976.[159] This covenant represented the first and only time in the history of U.S. territorial administration that the United States acquired an unincorporated territory based on an act of self-determination by the people of that territory.

The legislative history of the covenant reflects some of the same historical and legal factors that characterize the unincorporated territories discussed previously as well as some of the same confusion about the so-called commonwealth model for territorial administration.[160]

For example, the U.S. Senate Report recommending ratification of the covenant described the political status established under the covenant as follows:

> *The Character of the Relationship.*—Although described as a commonwealth, the relationship is territorial in nature with full sovereignty vested in the United States, and plenary legislative authority vested in the United States Congress. The authority of the latter is limited in a few areas through US federal restraint, i.e. by approval of the Covenant, the US government will agree not to exercise its authority in certain areas. The essential difference between the covenant and the usual territorial relationship (e.g. that with Guam) is the provision in the Covenant that the Marianas constitution and governmental structure will be a product of a Marianas constitutional convention, which follows the pattern of Puerto Rico, and not an organic act of the US Congress. Of particular significance, the Marianas commonwealth relationship, unlike the governmental structure of Guam or the Virgin Islands cannot be amended or terminated unilaterally by the US Congress. The Marianas commonwealth relationship will be significantly closer to the Guam territorial relationship than to the Puerto Rican commonwealth arrangement. The Marianas constitution must be consistent with applicable provisions of the US constitution, and with US treaties and laws applicable to the Marianas.[161]

This statement of legislative history is so internally inconsistent and contradictory as to be nearly unintelligible. The first sentence and last sentence are unambiguous. The United States has sovereign power over the CNMI, Congress can exercise plenary powers over the CNMI under the Territorial Clause, and local law in the CNMI is subject to the supremacy of federal law. Everything between the first and last sentences is either wrong or very confused.

First, it is true that Congress granted internal self-government to the CNMI and in its discretion under the territorial power adopted a statutory policy of voluntary restraint that includes a local privilege of consent before altering the CNMI's form of internal government. However, the federal courts would have no legal basis for enforcing such a policy of restraint on the power of Congress if Congress were by later statute to remove the restraints it earlier imposed on itself, thereby demonstrating the constitutional truism that Congress cannot cede its constitutional powers to a territory or bind a future Congress to a statutory policy on a political question such as territorial administration or status.[162]

Second, the covenant provisions that permitted the CNMI to adopt a local constitution are simply an advanced form of organic act authorizing an internal constitutional government in the territory, just like the federal statute authorizing local constitutions for Puerto Rico, Guam, and the Virgin Islands. In that respect, the CNMI is in a position no different from Guam and the Virgin Islands, except that those islands have not exercised their authority to adopt local constitutions under the organic acts applicable to them, while Puerto Rico and the CNMI have done so.[163] That is the reality that the passage quoted above from the U.S. Senate Report attempted to express. It is also the basis upon which the CNMI adopted a local constitution in accordance with Article II of the covenant and became an organized unincorporated territory of the United States. Finally, adoption of the local constitution under the CNMI covenant was also the basis upon which the United States terminated the UN Trusteeship with respect to the CNMI and assumed sovereign power over the CNMI.[164]

The CNMI is the only organized unincorporated territory of the United States that has no delegate or resident commissioner serving as a nonvoting member of the U.S. House of Representatives. Instead, the CNMI appoints a resident representative who is an employee and official of the local government and who resides in Washington to promote good relations between the federal and territorial governments.[165]

In addition, the CNMI is one of only two territories for which Congress has given a vague but intriguing suggestion with respect to future status resolution. In Section 1844 of Title 48 of the United States Code, Congress set forth a federal government promise that neither the CNMI nor Guam will suffer any reduction of federal funding, rights, or entitlements in the event of "political union" between the CNMI and Guam.[166] Guam and the CNMI have a common history and ethnic heritage. Based on the congressional recognition of these historical and ethnic ties, for Guam and the CNMI there is the possibility that unification could be a first step toward incorporation leading to statehood, a more credible goal if Guam and the CNMI combined to form a larger and more populous territory.

Although Guam has not yet adopted a local constitution and has not implemented any new policy on status since the federal government rejected its so-called commonwealth proposal,[167] the CNMI arguably has achieved the best "commonwealth" structure for local government of any U.S. territory. Nevertheless, the CNMI remains subject to the Territorial Clause power of Congress, and has not achieved full self-government, either as a state within the United States, possibly in union with Guam, or as a separate nation through independence or free association.

Remote Island Territories with No Form of Self-Government

In addition to the five "organized" unincorporated territories discussed above (American Samoa, Guam, Puerto Rico, the Northern Mariana Islands, and the Virgin Islands), the United States exercises supremacy and dominion over eleven small "unorganized" island territories—many of which are uninhabited or sparsely inhabited—for which federal law recognizes no form of self-government. These include three small islands (Bajo Nuevo, Navassa Island, and Serranilla Bank) in the Caribbean Sea and eight islands in the Pacific Ocean (Baker Island, Howland Island, Jarvis Island, Johnston Atoll, Kingman Reef, Midway Atoll, Palmyra Atoll,[168] and Wake Atoll).[169] All of these "unorganized" island territories are subject to congressional supervision under the Territorial Clause and statutory policies that apply to unincorporated territories in general.[170]

Notes

[1] The principles of the Northwest Ordinance for territorial incorporation into the Union were adapted to the particular circumstances of the following territories, each of which was admitted to statehood: Tennessee (1796), Ohio (1803), Louisiana (1812), Indiana (1816), Mississippi (1817), Illinois (1818), Alabama (1819), Missouri (1821), Arkansas (1836), Michigan (1837), Florida (1845), Iowa (1846), Wisconsin (1848), California (1850), Minnesota (1858), Oregon (1859), Kansas (1861), Nevada (1864), Nebraska (1867), Colorado (1876), North Dakota (1889), South Dakota (1889), Montana (1889), Washington (1889), Idaho (1890), Wyoming (1890), Utah (1896), Oklahoma (1907), New Mexico (1912), Arizona (1912), Alaska (1959), and Hawaii (1959). In addition, there were four new states formed from other states. These were Vermont (1791), Kentucky (1792), Maine (1820), and West Virginia (1863). Texas was an independent republic when admitted (1845), and California was under U.S. Army administration until admitted directly to the Union based on its local constitution.

[2] *Act of August 7, 1789*, ch. 8, *Statutes at Large of the United States of America* 1 (1789): 51 n.(a).

[3] Whitney T. Perkins, *Denial of Empire: The United States and Its Dependencies* (Leyden, The Netherlands: A.W. Sythoff, 1962), 14.

[4] *Act of August 7, 1789*, 1:50.

[5] Perkins, *Denial of Empire*, 14; Earl S. Pomeroy, *The Territories and the United States, 1861–1890: Studies in Colonial Administration* (Philadelphia: University of Pennsylvania Press, 1947).

[6] Perkins, *Denial of Empire*, 16–25.

[7] See Grupo de Investigadores Puertorriquenos, *Breakthrough from Colonialism: An Interdisciplinary Study of Statehood* (Río Piedras, Puerto Rico: Editorial de la Universidad de Puerto Rico, 1984), 1:687–741.

[8] Ibid., 2:745–1051.

[9] Perkins, *Denial of Empire*, 25–30. The Treaty of Peace was signed in Paris on December 10, 1898, and entered into force on April 11, 1899. "Treaty of Peace between the United States of America and the Kingdom of Spain," April 11, 1899, *United States Statutes at Large* 30:1754.

[10] The nine other "unorganized" U.S. territories are Navassa Island and Serranilla Bank in the Caribbean Sea and Baker Island, Howland Island, Jarvis Island, Johnston Atoll, Kingman Reef, Palmyra Atoll, and Wake Atoll in the Pacific Ocean.

[11] See *U.S. Code* 48 (2006), ch. 4, 8A, 10, 12, 13, 15, and 17.

[12] See *U.S. Code* 48 (2006), ch. 4, 8A, and 12 organizing local territorial governments in Puerto Rico, Guam, and Virgin Islands, respectively. See also

Rodriguez v. Popular Democratic Party, 457 U.S. 1 (1982); *United States v. Sanchez*, 992 F.2d 1143 (11th Cir. 1993).

[13] See *U.S. Code* 48 (2006), § 1469a–d, prescribing statutory policies common to territories.

[14] See, e.g., ibid., § 734.

[15] E.g., *Covenant to Establish a Commonwealth of the Northern Mariana Islands*, Sec. 104, Public Law 94-241 (1976), codified at *U.S. Code* 48 (2006), § 1801.

[16] See *U.S. Code* 48 (2006), § 1421a.

[17] Ibid., § 731b; *Covenant to Establish a Commonwealth of the Northern Mariana Islands*, Sec. 201, Public Law 94-241 (1976), codified at *U.S. Code* 48 (2006), § 1801.

[18] *United States v. Quinones*, 758 F.2d 40 (1st Cir. 1985); *United States v. Acosta-Martinez*, 252 F.3d 13 (1st Cir. 2001), *cert. denied*, 535 U.S. 906 (2002).

[19] See, e.g., *Covenant to Establish a Commonwealth of the Northern Mariana Islands*, Sec. 805, Public Law 94-241 (1976), codified at *U.S. Code* 48 (2006), § 1801, restricting land ownership in Mariana Islands to persons of native descent.

[20] *U.S. Code* 8 (2006), §§ 1402, 1407. See also *U.S. Code* 48 (2006), § 737, statutory policy extending the Privileges and Immunities of U.S. citizenship to Puerto Rico "as though Puerto Rico were a State of the Union"; § 738, incorporating Puerto Rico into the U.S. customs territory.

[21] See discussion of Puerto Rico's "foreign" status under *U.S. Code* 26 (2006), § 936; Lawrence A. Hunter, "Why Not Incorporate Puerto Rico into the U.S. Tax Code?" *Viewpoint*, 103 Tax Notes 917 (May 17, 2004); Joseph Pelzman, "Imported Capital Dependency as an Economic Development Strategy: The Failure of Distortionary Tax Policies in Puerto Rico," Center for Economic Research Discussion Paper No. 03-01, http://www.gwu.edu/~cer1/dis.html (December 2002); Susan M. Collins, Barry Bosworth, and Miguel A. Soto-Class, eds., *The Economy of Puerto Rico: Restoring Growth* (Washington, D.C.: Brookings Institution Press and the Center for the New Economy, 2006); Joint Committee on Taxation, *An Overview of the Special Tax Rules Related to Puerto Rico and an Analysis of the Tax and Economic Policy Implications of Recent Legislative Options*, (JCX-24-06), June 23, 2006; U.S. Government Accountability Office, *Puerto Rico Fiscal Relations with the Federal Government and Economic Trends during the Phaseout of the Possessions Tax Credit*, (GAO-06-541), May 2006.

[22] "Treaty of Peace between the United States of America and the Kingdom of Spain," April 11, 1899, *United States Statutes at Large* 30: 1754.

[23] Ibid., Art. I.

24 Ibid., Art. II, Art. III.

25 Ibid., Art. I, Art. XVI.

26 *Platt Amendment*, ch. 803, *U.S. Statutes at Large* 31 (1901): 895.

27 "Treaty of Peace," Art. III.

28 Ibid., Art. IX.

29 Perkins, *Denial of Empire*, 197–198.

30 Ibid., 201.

31 Ibid., 204–232.

32 See *Act of August 29, 1916 (Jones Act—Philippine Islands)*, ch. 416, *U.S. Statutes at Large* 39 (1916): 545 (Preamble).

33 Ibid.

34 Ibid.

35 Ibid., § 5.

36 Ibid., § 19.

37 Ibid., § 21.

38 Ibid., § 2.

39 *Tydings-McDuffie Act*, Public Law 73-127, *U.S. Statutes at Large* 48 (1934): 456.

40 See *U.S. Code* 48 (2006), §§ 1801, 731b. See also sections beginning on pages 15 and 28 of this chapter.

41 *Tydings-McDuffie Act*, § 2(a).

42 Ibid., § 5.

43 President, Proclamation, "Independence of the Philippines, Proclamation 2695," *Federal Register* 11 (July 1946): 7517, *U.S. Statutes at Large* 60: 1352.

44 *Rabang v. Boyd*, 353 U.S. 427 (1957); *Cabebe v. Acheson*, 183 F.2d 795 (9th Cir. 1950).

45 *Tydings-McDuffie Act*, § 14. Section 14 of the act provided: "Upon the final and complete withdrawal of American sovereignty over the Philippine Islands the immigration laws of the United States (including all the provisions thereof relating to persons ineligible to citizenship) shall apply to persons who were born in the Philippine Islands to the same extent as in the case of other foreign countries."

46 *Rabang v. Boyd*, 353 U.S. 427 (1957).

47 U.S. Constitution, art. 1, sec. 8. See *Rogers v. Bellei*, 401 U.S. 815 (1971), holding that those born or naturalized in a state acquire U.S. nationality and citizenship under the Fourteenth Amendment, but those who acquire it by

statute under the Naturalization Clause power in the same manner as before the Fourteenth Amendment was ratified, including those born to U.S. parents overseas and in U.S. territories, have a status that can be given and taken away subject to such conditions precedent and subsequent as Congress may in it discretion prescribe.

48 The combined effect of the *Bellei* and *Rabang* cases is to render inconsequential the distinction the lower court made in the *Cabebe* case between "nationality," "naturalization," and "citizenship." If statutory nationality is lost, statutory citizenship is lost as well, whether derived from statutory nationality or statutory naturalization (except where naturalization is in a state and thereby protected under the Fourteenth Amendment). Also, see discussion of U.S. citizenship renunciation cases in Puerto Rico in "Understanding U.S. Nationality and Citizenship in Puerto Rico," *Congressional Record* 144 (May 7, 1998): E801, clarifying the legal nature of U.S. nationality and citizenship in unincorporated territories.

49 "Treaty of Peace," Art. II.

50 Ibid., Art. IX.

51 House Committee on Resources, *Report on United States–Puerto Rico Political Status Act*, prepared by Mr. Young of Alaska, 105th Cong., 1st sess., 1997, H. Rep. 105-131, Part 1, 9–13.

52 See *United States–Puerto Rico Political Status Act*, H.R. 856, 105th Cong., 2d sess. (approved by the House of Representatives March 4, 1998).

53 *Act of April 12, 1900 (Foraker Act)*, ch. 191, *U.S. Statutes at Large* 31 (1900): 77.

54 *Foraker Act*, § 39; see also *U.S. Code* 48 (2006), § 891.

55 *Act of March 2, 1917 (Jones Act—Puerto Rico)*, ch. 145, *U.S. Statutes at Large* 39 (1917): 951. Five years later, the U.S. Supreme Court ruled that this extension of statutory U.S. citizenship to persons born in Puerto Rico did not incorporate, or extend the U.S. Constitution of its own force to, that territory. See discussion of *Balzac* ruling in the section beginning on page 1 of the Introduction.

56 *Act of July 3, 1950*, Public Law 81-600, *U.S. Statutes at Large* 64 (1950): 319.

57 Ibid., §§ 2, 3, codified at *U.S. Code* 48 (2006), § 731(c), (d).

58 See *U.S. Code* 48 (2006), § 731(c) (Historical and Statutory Notes).

59 Ibid.

60 Ibid.

61 Ibid.

62 *Act of July 3, 1952*, Public Law 82-447, *U.S. Statutes at Large* 66 (1952): 327.

63 The Constitution of the Commonwealth of Puerto Rico is available at http://welcome.topuertorico.org/constitu.shtml.

[64] See *United States v. Sanchez*, 992 F.2d 1143 (11th Cir. 1993).

[65] See *United States v. Acosta-Martinez*, 252 F.3d 13 (1st Cir. 2001) (reversing district court decision reported at 106 F. Supp. 2d 311 (D.P.R. 2000)).

[66] The term "commonwealth" is used throughout this book to refer to local territorial governments given that appellation under local or federal law and in some cases to proposals for new forms of government in the territories that do not exist under current law. The term appears in quotation marks throughout this book because reference to a territory as a "commonwealth" has no legal meaning or effect. This term does not define the political status of the body politic adopting it or the constitutional or legal relationship of such a political subdivision to other political subdivisions or to the federal government. Just as a state that calls itself a commonwealth (e.g., the Commonwealth of Pennsylvania) has the same political status as all other states, an incorporated or unincorporated terrority that calls itself a commonwealth has the same political status as other incorporated or unincorporated territories, respectively.

[67] Perkins, *Denial of Empire,* 146–160.

[68] Constitutional Convention of Puerto Rico, *Resolution No. 34* (July 10, 1952), reprinted in *Documents on the Constitutional Relationship of Puerto Rico and the United States* (Washington, D.C.: Puerto Rico Federal Affairs Administration, 1988).

[69] See *U.S. Code* 48 (2006), § 731(d) (Historical and Statutory Notes).

[70] See annotation to Article VII, Section 3 of the Constitution of the Commonwealth of Puerto Rico, stating that referendum ratifying amendments to constitution was conducted on November 4, 1952, available at http://welcome.topuertorico.org/constitu.shtml; see also *U.S. Code* 48 (2006), § 732 (repealed) (Historical and Statutory Notes).

[71] G.A. Res. 748, U.N. GAOR, 8th Sess., Supp. No. 17, U.N. Doc A/2630 (1953).

[72] Ibid.

[73] House Committee on Resources, *Report on United States–Puerto Rico Political Status Act*, prepared by Mr. Young of Alaska, 105th Cong., 1st sess., 1997, H. Rep. 105-131, Part 1, 65–66 (Appendix A, ¶21).

[74] See, e.g., *United States v. Sanchez,* 992 F.2d 1143 (11th Cir. 1993).

[75] See *Senate Resolution 279*, 105th Cong., 2d sess. (September 17, 1998).

[76] See discussion of H.R. 856 on page 19 of this chapter.

[77] The most recent instruments of federal policy recognizing the unresolved status of Puerto Rico include Executive Order no. 13183, *Federal Register* 65 (December 2000): 82889 (entitled *Establishment of the President's Task Force on Puerto Rico's Status)*, which implements the policy set forth in the *Memorandum*

of the President on Puerto Rico, Federal Register 57 (November 1992): 57093 (reprinted at *U.S. Code* 48 (2006), § 734 (Historical and Statutory Notes).

78 See U.S. Deputy Assistant Attorney General to Special Representative for Guam Commonwealth, July 28, 1994, *Memorandum Regarding Mutual Consent Provisions in the Guam Commonwealth Legislation* ("DOJ Memorandum"), reprinted in House Committee on Resources, Subcommittee on Native American & Insular Affairs, *United States–Puerto Rico Political Status Act: Hearing on H.R. 3024*, 104th Cong., 2d sess., 1996, No. 104-87, 158–169.

79 See DOJ Memorandum, ibid., reviewing history of federal legal policy on territorial status in light of *Bowen v. Agencies Opposed to Soc. Sec. Entrapment*, 477 U.S. 41 (1986).

80 Puerto Rico's status as a territory under U.S. sovereignty is defined by federal statutes approved by Congress in the exercise of its powers under the Territorial Clause, including Title 48, Chapter 4 of the U.S. Code, and by federal decisional law. Thus, only changes in federal law will end Puerto Rico's current territorial status in favor of a nonterritorial status.

81 House Committee on Resources, *The Results of the 1998 Puerto Rico Plebiscite*, prepared by Chairman Don Young and Senior Democratic Member George Miller, 106th Cong., 1st sess., 1999, Committee Print, Appendix D states: "Following conferral of United States citizenship on persons born in Puerto Rico in 1917 (39 Stat. 961) and establishment of internal self-government under a locally-adopted constitution approved by Congress (64 Stat. 319), three political status votes have been conducted in Puerto Rico, but without federal authorization. The legal definitions of status options and the manner in which such options were presented on the ballot in each vote were determined through the internal constitutional process of Puerto Rico and prescribed by local law. The results of these votes were as follows:

Dates and Results of Puerto Rico Political Status Plebiscite Votes*

Ballot Options	July 23, 1967	November 14, 1993	December 13, 1998
Commonwealth	60.5%	48.6%	0.01%
Statehood	38.9	46.4	46.5
Independence	0.5	4.5	2.5
Free association	*	*	0.02
None of the above	*	*	50.2

* Only the December 13, 1998, vote included ballot options of "free association" and "none of the above."

82 See discussion on pages 22–23 of this chapter.

83 *The Results of the 1998 Puerto Rico Plebiscite*, Appendix D. See House Committee on Resources, *Report on United States–Puerto Rico Political Status*

Act, prepared by Mr. Young of Alaska, 105th Cong., 1st sess., 1997, H. Rep. 105-131, Part 1, 20–22.

[84] *The Results of the 1998 Puerto Rico Plebiscite,* Appendix D.

[85] Legislature of Puerto Rico, *Concurrent Resolution 62* (December 14, 1994), available in House Committee on Resources, *Report on United States–Puerto Rico Political Status Act*, prepared by Mr. Young of Alaska, 104th Cong., 2d sess., 1996, H. Rep. 104-713, Part 1, Appendix I.

[86] Legislature of Puerto Rico, *Concurrent Resolution 2* (January 23, 1997), available in House Committee on Resources, *Report on United States–Puerto Rico Political Status Act*, prepared by Mr. Young of Alaska, 105th Cong., 1st sess., 1997, H. Rep. 105-131, Part 1, Appendix B.

[87] *United States–Puerto Rico Political Status Act*, H.R. 856, 105th Cong., 2d sess., § 4 (approved by the House of Representatives March 4, 1998).

[88] *Senate Resolution 472*, 105th Cong., 1st sess. (March 19, 1997).

[89] House Committee on Resources, *Puerto Rico–United States Bilateral Pact of Non-Territorial Permanent Union and Guaranteed Citizenship Act: Hearing on H.R. 4751*, 107th Cong., 1st sess., 2000, Committee Print 107-C. See chapter 5 for a discussion of this "enhanced commonwealth" proposal.

[90] *Senate Resolution 279*, 105th Cong., 2d sess. (September 17, 1998).

[91] *The Results of the 1998 Puerto Rico Plebiscite,* Appendix A and D.

[92] Ibid., Appendix D.

[93] Ibid.

[94] See *Igartúa de la Rosa v. United States*, 417 F.3d 145, 170–179 (1st Cir. 2005) (Torruella, J. dissenting).

[95] "Treaty of Peace," Art. II, Art. V.

[96] Perkins, *Denial of Empire,* 300–307.

[97] Ibid., 307–308.

[98] *U.S. Code* 8 (2006), § 1407.

[99] *Organic Act of Guam*, ch. 512, *U.S. Statutes at Large* 64 (1950): 384, codified as amended at *U.S. Code* 48 (2006), §§ 1421–1424.

[100] *Act of October 21, 1976*, Public Law 94-584, *U.S. Statutes at Large* 90 (1976): 2899.

[101] *Act of July 3, 1950*, Public Law 81-600, *U.S. Statutes at Large* 64 (1950): 319, codified at *U.S. Code* 48 (2006), §§ 731b et seq.

[102] *Act of March 24, 1976*, Public Law 94-241, *U.S. Statutes at Large* 90 (1976): 263. See section beginning on page 28 of this chapter.

[103] *Act of October 21, 1976*, § 2.

[104] See discussion on page 17 of this chapter.

[105] See Legislature of Guam, *Resolution No. 85* (September 15, 1997), reprinted in House Committee on Resources, *Report on Virgin Islands and Guam Constitutional Self-Government Act of 2000*, prepared by Mr. Young of Alaska, 106th Cong., 2d sess., 2000, H. Rep. 106-745, Appendix, discussing 1979 draft Constitution of Guam and requesting the U.S. Congress to confirm that adoption of a local constitution would "not preclude or prejudice the further exercise in the future . . . of the right of self-determination regarding the ultimate political status" of Guam. See also, House Committee on Resources, *Report on House Resolution 494*, prepared by Mr. Young of Alaska, 105th Cong., 2d sess., 1998, H. Rep. 105-751, providing that the House of Representatives "reaffirm its commitment to increase self-government consistent with self-determination for the people of Guam"; U.S. House of Representatives, *Sense of the House Regarding Guam*, October 13, 1998. (Mr. Young of Alaska stated that "the people of Guam . . . can be assured that the adoption of a constitution as authorized by Congress will not prejudice or preclude their right of self-determination and the fundamental right to seek a change in their political status in the future.")

[106] See *Guam Commonwealth Act*, H.R. 100, 105th Cong., 1st sess. (January 7, 1997). See also *House Resolution 494*, 105th Cong., 2d sess. (October 13, 1998).

[107] See section beginning on page 27 of this chapter. See also House Committee on Resources, *Guam Commonwealth Act: Hearings on H.R. 100*, 105th Cong., 1st sess., 1997 (statement of Antonio R. Unpingco, Speaker and Senator (R) of the Twenty-Fourth Guam Legislature), http://resourcescommittee.house.gov/archives/105cong/fullcomm/oct29.97/unpingco.htm.

[108] *Act of April 10, 1972*, Public Law 92-271, *U.S. Statutes at Large* 86 (1972): 118, codified at *U.S. Code* 48 (2006), § 1711.

[109] House Committee on Resources, *Guam Commonwealth Act: Hearings on H.R. 100*, 105th Cong., 1st sess., 1997.

[110] DOJ Memorandum, 158–169. See also House Committee on Resources, *Report on United States–Puerto Rico Political Status Act*, prepared by Mr. Young of Alaska, 104th Cong., 2d sess., 1996, H. Rep. 104-713, Part 1, 21–22.

[111] DOJ Memorandum, 1–2 & n.2.

[112] DOJ Memorandum, 12.

[113] Robert Friedman, "Guam Commonwealth Proposals Killed," *San Juan Star*, October 30, 1997. The Clinton administration's rejection of mutual consent and binding commonwealth was followed with interest in Puerto Rico, especially the remarks of Congressman Neil Abercrombie (D-Hawaii) at the Guam hearings quoted in the same news article cited here, including his observation: "We learned in Puerto Rico that you can't write a definition of

commonwealth to suit yourself . . . . Some people in Puerto Rico don't understand this. You cannot pick and choose which laws you want applied to you."

[114] Ibid.

[115] John Omicinski, "No Commonwealth," *Pacific Daily News*, October 31, 1997.

[116] See discussion of Guam-CNMI unification as possible step in status resolution process on page 31 of this chapter.

[117] Alaska was ceded to the United States by Russia on March 30, 1867, under the "Treaty of Cession of the Russian Possessions in North America to the United States," *United States Statutes at Large* 15:539. Hawaii was annexed by a joint resolution of Congress signed by President McKinley on July 7, 1898. *Joint Resolution to Provide for Annexing the Hawaiian Islands to the United States*, 55th Cong., 2d sess., *U.S. Statutes at Large* 30 (1898): 750.

[118] See discussion of the *Insular Cases* beginning on page 46 of chapter 2 and the discussion of *Rassmussen v. United States* and *Hawaii v. Mankichi* beginning on page 48 of chapter 2.

[119] "Treaty of Cession of the Russian Possessions," Art. III.

[120] *Rassmussen v. United States*, 197 U.S. 516 (1905).

[121] *Act of April 30, 1900*, ch. 339, *U.S. Statutes at Large* 31 (1900): 141.

[122] *Hawaii v. Mankichi*, 190 U.S. 197 (1903).

[123] Ibid.

[124] See discussion on page 52 of chapter 2 regarding why the Supreme Court's holding in *Balzac* cannot be reconciled with the Court's holding in *Rassmussen*.

[125] *U.S. Code* 48 (2006), § 1661. See Perkins, *Denial of Empire*, 271; "Convention between the United States, Germany, and Great Britain to Adjust Amicably the Questions between the Three Governments in Respect to the Samoan Group of Islands," December 2, 1899, available in U.S. Department of State, *Foreign Relations of the United States* (Washington, D.C.: Government Printing Office, 1899), 667.

[126] *U.S. Code* 48 (2006), § 1661(c).

[127] Executive Order no. 10264, *Federal Register* 16 (June 1951): 6419 (reprinted at *U.S. Code* 48 (2006), § 1662).

[128] U.S. Department of the Interior, *Secretarial Order No. 3009* (June 27, 1978).

[129] *U.S. Code* 48 (2006), § 1662a.

[130] *U.S. Code* 48 (2006), § 1731.

[131] *U.S. Code* 8 (2006), § 1408.

[132] *U.S. Code* 48 (2006), § 1661(c); "Executive Order no. 10264."

[133] The local constitution was promulgated by the U.S. Secretary of the Interior, and can be amended only by Congress, as provided at *U.S. Code* 48 (2006), § 1662a.

[134] *U.S. Code* 48 (2006), § 1661(b).

[135] Perkins, *Denial of Empire,* 277, 289–291.

[136] "Treaty between the United States and Denmark for Cession of the Danish West Indies," August 4, 1916, *United States Statutes at Large* 39: 1706; see also Perkins, *Denial of Empire,* 166.

[137] *Act of March 3, 1917,* Public Law 64-389, *U.S. Statutes at Large* 39 (1917): 1132.

[138] Perkins, *Denial of Empire,* 173–174.

[139] *U.S. Code* 8 (2006), § 1406.

[140] Perkins, *Denial of Empire,* 175.

[141] *Organic Act of the Virgin Islands of the United States,* Public Law 74-749, *U.S. Statutes at Large* 49 (1936): 1807.

[142] *Revised Organic Act of the Virgin Islands,* Public Law 83-517, *U.S. Statutes at Large* 68 (1954): 497.

[143] Ibid., § 5.

[144] Ibid., § 2.

[145] Perkins, *Denial of Empire,* 178 (discussing Senate Report 1271).

[146] *Virgin Islands Elective Governor Act,* Public Law 90-496, *U.S. Statutes at Large* 82 (1968): 837.

[147] *Act of April 10, 1972,* Public Law 92-271, *U.S. Statutes at Large* 86 (1972): 118.

[148] *Act of October 21, 1976,* Public Law 94-584, *U.S. Statutes at Large* 90 (1976): 2899.

[149] *Joint Resolution to Approve a Constitution for the United States Virgin Islands,* Public Law 97-21, *U.S. Statutes at Large* 95 (1981): 105 (discussed in *U.S. Code* 48 (2006), § 1541 (Historical and Statutory Notes); House Committee on Resources, *Report on Virgin Islands and Guam Constitutional Self-Government Act of 2000,* prepared by Mr. Young of Alaska, 106th Cong., 2d sess., 2000, H. Rep. 106-745.

[150] "Trusteeship Agreement for the Former Japanese Mandated Islands," July 18, 1947, *United States Statutes at Large* 61:3301, T.I.A.S. No. 1665, 8 U.N.T.S. 189. See Howard L. Hills, *Compact of Free Association for Micronesia: Constitutional and International Law Issues,* 18 Int'l Law. 583 (1984).

[151] Executive Order no. 9875, *Federal Register* 12 (July 1947): 4837.

[152] Executive Order no. 10264, *Federal Register* 16 (June 1951): 6419. Puerto Rico is the only U.S. territory not within the cognizance of the Department of the Interior's Office of Insular Affairs.

[153] "Trusteeship Agreement," Art. 9.

[154] Ibid., Art. 11.

[155] U.S. Department of the Interior, *Secretarial Order No. 3039* (April 25, 1979).

[156] *Compact of Free Association Act of 1985*, Public Law 99-239, *U.S. Statutes at Large* 99 (1986): 1770. See Howard L. Hills, *Compact of Free Association for Micronesia: Constitutional and International Law Issues*, 18 Int'l Law. 583 (1984).

[157] Although the president of the United States declared that the trusteeship was no longer in effect by issuing a proclamation to that effect on November 3, 1986 (President, "Proclamation 5564," sec. 1, *Federal Register* 51 (November 1986): 40399), after a U.S. Claims Court agreed that the trusteeship could not be terminated, under international law, without UN Security Council approval, *Juda v. United States,* 13 Cl. Ct. 667 (1987), the political branches of the U.S. government and other relevant parties sought and received such approval from the UN Security Council when it approved Resolution 956 on November 10, 1994. See also section beginning on page 67 of chapter 3.

[158] An update on free association as recognized under international law and by the United States in the case of the former Trust territories can be found at Howard L. Hills, *Free Association for Micronesia and the Marshall Islands: A Transitional Political Status Model,* 27 Haw. L. Rev. 1 (2004).

[159] "Covenant to Establish a Commonwealth of the Northern Mariana Islands (CNMI) in Political Union with the United States of America" ("CNMI Covenant"), March 24, 1976, Public Law 94-241, *United States Statutes at Large* 90 (1976): 263.

[160] It appears that only the Philippine "commonwealth" model (see discussion in section beginning on page 12 of this chapter), which implemented a clear policy of autonomy leading to sovereign nationhood, was unambiguous about the purpose and nature of its "commonwealth" structure.

[161] Senate Committee on Interior and Insular Affairs, *Report on the Covenant to Establish a Commonwealth of the Northern Mariana Islands,* 94th Cong., 1st sess., 1975, S. Rep. 94-433, 15.

[162] See DOJ Memorandum. See also *United States v. Sanchez,* 992 F.2d 1143, 1152–1153 (11th Cir. 1993), stating that "Congress may unilaterally repeal the Puerto Rican Constitution or the Puerto Rican Federal Relations Act and replace them with any rules or regulations of its choice."

[163] See sections beginning on pages 15, 21, and 26 of this chapter.

[164] President, "Proclamation 5564," *Federal Register* 51 (November 1986): 40399.

[165] "CNMI Covenant," Art. IX.

[166] *Act of December 24, 1980*, Public Law 96-597, *U.S. Statutes at Large* 94 (1980): 3480, Title VI, § 602.

[167] See section on Guam beginning on page 21 of this chapter.

[168] Interestingly, Palmyra Atoll was part of the incorporated territory of Hawaii, but was separated from Hawaii by a provision added to the *Hawaii Statehood Act*, Public Law 86-3, *U.S. Statutes at Large* 73 (1959): 4, § 2.

[169] Palmyra Atoll was annexed with Hawaii on July 7, 1898. *Joint Resolution to Provide for Annexing the Hawaiian Islands to the United States*, 55th Cong., 2d sess., *U.S. Statutes at Large* 30 (1898): 750. See Executive Order no. 8682, *Federal Register* 6 (February 1941): 1015; Executive Order no. 10967, *Federal Register* 26 (October 1961): 9667.

Wake Atoll is an unoccupied island that was annexed by the United States on January 17, 1899. See "Executive Order no. 8682"; Executive Order no. 11048, *Federal Register* 27 (September 1962): 8851.

Midway Atoll was occupied by the United States on August 28, 1867. See "Executive Order no. 8682"; "Executive Order no. 11048"; Executive Order no. 13022, *Federal Register* 61 (October 1996): 56875.

The other islands were annexed under the *Guano Islands Act of 1856*, ch. 164, *U.S. Statutes at Large* 11 (1856): 119 (codified at *U.S. Code* 48 (2006): §§ 1411–1419): Baker Island (October 28, 1856); Jarvis Island (October 28, 1856); Navassa Island (October 31, 1858); Howland Island (December 3, 1858); Johnston Atoll (September 6, 1859); Kingman Reef (February 8, 1860); Bajo Nuevo (November 22, 1869); Serranilla Bank (September 8, 1879, and September 13, 1880).

[170] See *U.S. Code* 48 (2006), §§ 1469a–d, prescribing statutory policies common to territories.

CHAPTER TWO

CONSTITUTIONAL ISSUES RELATING TO THE TREATMENT OF U.S. TERRITORIES

OVERVIEW OF RELEVANT PROVISIONS

Several provisions of the U.S. Constitution bear on the treatment of U.S. territories and their residents. The most significant are the following:

- *The Territorial Clause*

  "The Congress shall have Power to dispose of and make all needful Rules and Regulations respecting the Territory or other Property belonging to the United States . . . ."—U.S. Constitution, art. 4, sec. 3, cl. 2.

- *The Naturalization Clause*

  "The Congress shall have Power . . . [t]o establish an uniform Rule of Naturalization . . . ."—U.S. Constitution, art. 1, sec. 8, cl. 4.

- *The Equal Protection Clause*

  "No State shall . . . deny to any person within its jurisdiction the equal protection of the laws."—U.S. Constitution, amend. 14, sec. 1.

- *The Due Process Clause*

  "No person shall . . . be deprived of life, liberty, or property, without due process of law . . . ."—U.S. Constitution, amend. 5.

  "No State shall . . . deprive any person of life, liberty, or property, without due process of law . . . ." —U.S. Constitution, amend. 14, sec. 1.

- *The Supremacy Clause*

  "This Constitution, and the Laws of the United States which shall be made in Pursuance thereof; and all Treaties made, or which shall be made, under the Authority of the United States, shall be the supreme Law of the Land; and the Judges in every State shall be bound thereby, any Thing in the Constitution or Laws of any State to the Contrary notwithstanding." —U.S. Constitution, art. 6, cl. 2.

- *The Electoral College*

  "The executive Power shall be vested in a President of the United States of America. He shall . . . be elected, as follows:

  Each **State** shall appoint, in such Manner as the Legislature thereof may direct, a Number of Electors . . . ." —U.S. Constitution, art. 2, sec. 1 [emphasis added].

- *The Members of Congress*

  "The House of Representatives shall be composed of Members chosen every second Year by the People of the several States . . . ." —U.S. Constitution, art. 1, sec. 2, cl. 1.

  "The Senate of the United States shall be composed of two Senators from each State . . . ." —U.S. Constitution, art. 1, sec. 3, cl. 1.

This chapter discusses how the Supreme Court has applied and interpreted these provisions of the Constitution when dealing with the legal rights of U.S. territories and their citizens.

SUPREME COURT DECISIONS RELATING TO THE TREATMENT OF U.S. TERRITORIES

The Constitution, through the Territorial Clause, explicitly grants to Congress the power to determine how to regulate and "dispose of" all U.S. territory. As mentioned previously, the first Congress adopted the Northwest Ordinance as the template for the treatment and ultimate disposition of U.S. territories. The Northwest Ordinance assumed that a geographic area's designation as a "territory" of the United States was a temporary status that would ultimately lead to incorporation of that territory into the Union as a state.[1] The Northwest Ordinance represented a "compact" that incrementally extended the Constitution's promise of equality and government by consent of the governed to the citizens of all territories claimed under U.S. sovereignty, embodying a solemn commitment that territorial incorporation would culminate in full enfranchisement, equal citizenship rights, and government by consent of the governed through admission to the Union.[2]

The *Insular Cases*

During the years following the end of the Spanish-American War in 1898, a new model of territorial administration emerged, not so much through measures promulgated by Congress in the exercise of its power over territories under the Territorial Clause as through a series of U.S. Supreme Court decisions known as the *Insular Cases.*[3] In the *Insular Cases*, the Supreme Court held that federal courts could determine that certain territories (including Puerto Rico) were not incorporated in the tradition of the Northwest Ordinance and should be considered "unincorporated" territories.[4]

The unincorporated territory doctrine of the *Insular Cases* departed significantly from the Northwest Ordinance model and its anticolonial tradition of territorial incorporation. The Supreme Court justified this departure, in part, on the fact that the new territories acquired from Spain were inhabited by "alien races."[5] As it had for other territories, Congress had enacted legislation—in this case the Foraker Act—to prescribe the organization of government for the newly acquired territory of Puerto Rico[6] without defining a policy for resolution of Puerto Rico's ultimate political status. In the course of construing that organic legislation, the Court essentially invented a new political status policy by ruling that Congress intended something other than incorporation and that other something was "unincorporated territory" status.

A pivotal element of the Court's ruling that the organic act of Congress created a new political status was that the legislation embodied "an implied denial of the rights of the inhabitants to American citizenship until Congress by further action shall signify its assent thereto."[7] Based on the Court's perception of the *implied* meaning of early congressional policy on citizenship in Puerto Rico, the Court imposed a judicially determined and quite *explicit* political status policy denominating Puerto Rico as an "unincorporated territory."

The political and historical context for the *Insular Cases* decisions should not be ignored. At the time, both Congress and the Supreme Court were deeply divided over whether the Constitution allowed the United States to govern an alien population in a territory not incorporated into the national political system.[8] Those who declared themselves "imperialists" argued that the United States had the same right as other nations to acquire and govern foreign territories without incorporating them into the Union.[9] Those who opposed this departure from the anticolonial tradition of territorial incorporation labeled themselves "anti-imperialists" and made arguments against imperial rule. The anti-imperialist view arguably can be reconciled as consistent with the idea that even the "Manifest Destiny" doctrine that lay behind earlier continental expansion was neither colonialist nor imperialist, as long as the path of full self-government and equality within the American federal system was open through the incorporation process or through separate nationhood for any territory not so incorporated.[10]

In *Downes v. Bidwell*, a majority of the Supreme Court adopted the "imperialist" theory of national sovereignty as it related to the territories.[11] To sustain its ruling, the Court's majority presented an expansive theory of Territorial Clause power that in most respects placed unincorporated territories outside the constitutional order of the federal system, unless and until the Congress or the courts determined that a particular constitutional principle must be applied or that the territory should be incorporated into the Union in the anticolonial tradition of the Northwest Ordinance.[12] The Court's majority reasoned that it was a necessary feature of America's national sovereignty for the federal government to rule people of unincorporated territories, who while in that status lacked legally recognized inalienable rights or inherent sovereignty. The Court's majority held that these people could exercise local rights and powers of self-government only as allowed through the federal political or legal process, permissively and revocably, at the discretion of Congress.[13] Again, the "alien race" of the inhabitants in the far-flung territories acquired from Spain, as well as what the decision of Congress not to immediately extend U.S. citizenship to the culturally diverse populations implied to the Court, was pivotal to the reasoning behind the bold imperialist doctrine formulated by the Court.

The ruling in *Downes* effectively curtailed the political debate between the imperialists and anti-imperialists in Congress by interpreting the Foraker Act,[14] which Congress had adopted for civilian administration of Puerto Rico, to mean that Congress intended something other than incorporation for Puerto Rico. In *Downes*, the Court declared that the "American Empire," as referred to decades earlier by Chief Justice John Marshall during the continental expansion westward, now included not only incorporated territories in the tradition of the Northwest Ordinance, but also territories acquired during America's experiment with conquest and imperial rule over foreign peoples under U.S. national protection.[15] In the view of the Supreme Court, the present and future civil, legal, and political status of the people in these territories could be determined by federal statutory or decisional law, without having to contend with the issue of whether the U.S. Constitution applied to such territories by its own force, as in the case of incorporated territories.[16]

Even though the unincorporated territory doctrine of the *Insular Cases* was a departure from the anticolonial tradition of territorial incorporation, it is significant to note that at least initially the Supreme Court did not apply that doctrine to territories with U.S. citizen populations. Even for noncitizens in the unincorporated territories, the political limbo of this new Court-created status presumably would be "temporary" (like the territorial status contemplated by the Northwest Ordinance) until Congress determined the terms for territorial incorporation or transition to separate national sovereignty.[17]

Rassmussen and *Mankichi*

At about the same time that the Supreme Court was creating the unincorporated territory status for territories acquired from Spain, the Court held that Congress had intended to grant U.S. citizenship to territorial inhabitants of all races and cultural origins in the territories of Alaska and Hawaii. Consequently, the Court ruled that the processes of annexation and naturalization that Congress had approved for these territories signified that, unlike Puerto Rico and other territories acquired from Spain, Alaska and Hawaii were on the path of incorporation in the anticolonial tradition of the Northwest Ordinance and would be eligible for admission to the Union at a time to be determined by Congress.[18]

In *Rassmussen v. United States*, the Court concluded that Congress had intended for Alaska to be placed on the path toward incorporation because the Treaty of Cession with Russia, by which the United States acquired sovereignty over Alaska, provided that "[t]he inhabitants of the ceded territory shall be admitted to the enjoyment of all the rights, advantages and immunities of *citizens* of the United States . . . ."[19] In *Hawaii v. Mankichi*, the Court determined that Hawaii was incorporated in 1900 when Congress adopted an organic act that extended U.S. citizenship to the citizens of Hawaii and "formally extended" the U.S. Constitution to the Hawaiian Islands.[20] By contrast, the Treaty of Peace with Spain provided only that Congress would determine the "civil rights and political status of the native inhabitants of the territories [including Puerto Rico] hereby ceded to the United States," and when Congress passed the

Foraker Act in 1900 to govern the administration of Puerto Rico, it said nothing about U.S. citizenship for the residents of Puerto Rico.[21]

Gonzales and the Status of Territorial Residents as "Nationals," Not "Citizens"

Again it should be emphasized that a linchpin of the Supreme Court's rulings in the *Insular Cases* was that incorporation and extension of the U.S. Constitution to unincorporated territories were not intended or warranted because the residents of such territories were not U.S. citizens. In *Gonzales v. Williams*, the Supreme Court held that, although territorial residents were not citizens, neither were they aliens under federal immigration laws.[22] Instead, the Court invented a new class of persons "who live in the peace of the dominion" under U.S. national protection, leaving Congress to determine further the "political status and civil rights" of these residents of the territories acquired from Spain.[23]

Arguably, this limbo status for noncitizen "nationals" was a practical response to the necessity of governing noncitizens in newly acquired overseas territories until a more evolved political status policy could be devised. However, the *Gonzales* decision also demonstrates that once the courts start making political and social policy, they often have to make yet more political and social policy to sustain those court-created policies that are not sustained by measures adopted by the political branches of government.

In making the distinction between citizens and nationals in *Gonzales*, however, the Court was aided by the fact that Congress had previously adopted a distinction between citizens and "nationals" when it had declared inhabitants of the Philippines territory "citizens of the Philippine Islands" and nationals "entitled to the protection of the United States."[24] Being a "national" but not a "citizen" of the United States under federal statutory law does not confer or secure full and equal Fourteenth Amendment nationality, as the thousands of resident U.S. nationals involuntarily returned to the Philippines after Philippine independence was granted were to learn the hard way.[25] U.S. nationals have been held to owe allegiance to the United States,[26] but not to have all the rights of U.S. citizens, giving an ominous meaning to the quasi-legal maxim that "all citizens are nationals, but not all nationals are citizens."

What that means in the territorial law context is that under the Supreme Court's decisions in *Downes* and *Gonzales*, the United States institutionalized and legalized the exercise of sovereignty over persons in the territories who as "nationals" were *subjects* of U.S. sovereignty, but did not have citizenship or the rights of citizens except as provided by Congress. This less-than-equal form of statutory U.S. nationality still applies to residents of American Samoa and a narrow class of persons born in the Northern Mariana Islands.[27]

The broader and long-term significance of this court-driven legal, political, and social policy became even more apparent after the United States began granting statutory U.S. citizenship to the inhabitants of the unincorporated territories of Puerto Rico, Guam, the U.S. Virgin Islands, and the Northern Mariana Islands under the Naturalization Clause. Granting statutory citizenship under the Naturalization Clause is a necessary practice that provides statutory citizenship for those who do not automatically acquire it by operation of the Fourteenth Amendment based on birth or naturalization in a state—for example, the children of U.S. citizens born in foreign countries.[28] However, the combined effect of *Balzac v. Porto Rico* (discussed below), in which the Court enabled Congress to govern Puerto Rico after statutory U.S. citizenship was conferred in the same manner as when it was inhabited by nationals but not citizens under the *Insular Cases*, and *Rogers v. Bellei,* ruling that U.S. citizenship acquired by statute enacted under the Naturalization Clause can be conferred or terminated by operation of conditions, limitations, or restrictions imposed by Congress,[29] has enabled Congress to treat citizens in unincorporated territories as a subclass of citizens subject to discrimination not allowed among citizens in the states.

Unless interpreted differently in subsequent Supreme Court rulings, the combined result of this body of decisional law appears to be the following:

- The provisions of the U.S. Constitution, including the Fourteenth Amendment citizenship rights provision, do not apply in the unincorporated territories unless Congress expressly extends those provisions, which as a matter of general territorial policy it has not.
- Even where Congress does extend the Fourteenth Amendment or other provisions of the U.S. Constitution to the territories, that does not mean the federal constitution then applies to the territory of its own force, and would not prevent a later Congress from reversing that statutory policy.
- U.S. nationality and U.S. citizenship can be conferred in a territory by statute, but that statutory policy can be terminated by Congress at any time.

In the context of political status resolution leading to separate sovereign nationhood, those individuals who acquired U.S. nationality and citizenship based on birth in a territory could be repatriated or required to make an election of allegiance and citizenship between the United States and the former territory upon its succession to nationhood.[30]

Balzac v. Porto Rico: The *Dred Scott* Case of the 1920s?

The decision of the Supreme Court in the *Insular Cases* to define a new "unincorporated" territory status allowed Congress to govern noncitizen subjects "under the national protection of the U.S." or "nationals" under U.S. sovereignty without extending U.S. citizenship or equal rights under the U.S. Constitution. Incorporation came with U.S. citizenship and application of the U.S. Constitution, while unincorporated territory status did not. That was the new imperialist order for territorial administration, created by the Court in the vacuum created by the lack of a clear policy and attendant silence of Congress on the ultimate political status it intended for the territories acquired from Spain.

But an explicit premise of the *Insular Cases* was that the political and legal condition defined by the Court as unincorporated territory status applied only to *noncitizen* populations, and that unincorporated territory status was temporary until Congress determined how to "dispose" of a territory, through conferral of U.S. citizenship and incorporation leading to statehood, or by succession to separate nationhood.

Unfortunately, this balancing of constitutional principles and political realities in the *Insular Cases* was overlooked, ignored, or abandoned by the U.S. Supreme Court almost two decades later when it decided *Balzac v. Porto Rico*.[31] In yet another bold incursion into the realm of territorial policy reserved to Congress under the Territorial Clause, the Court ruled in *Balzac* that even the decision by Congress to confer U.S. citizenship on the population of a territory (in this case, Puerto Rico)[32] did not put that territory on the path toward incorporation or extend to its residents the protections of the Constitution.[33] In the Court's view, the unincorporated status of Puerto Rico under the doctrine of the *Insular Cases* had been clear when Congress granted residents of Puerto Rico citizenship in 1917, and the Court found no features in the Act conferring citizenship from which they could infer that Congress intended to incorporate Puerto Rico into the United States.[34] The Court stated that "[i]ncorporation has always been a step, and an important one, leading to statehood .... [and] it is reasonable to assume that when such a step is taken it will be begun and taken by Congress deliberately and with a clear declaration of purpose, and not left . . . [to] mere inference or construction."[35]

As a result, the Court held, the status and rights of U.S. citizens in an unincorporated territory, such as Puerto Rico, were to be determined by Congress in the exercise of its powers under the Territorial Clause, and were not defined or protected by direct application of the Constitution.[36] The only limit on the discretion of Congress in governing U.S. citizens in unincorporated territories, in the Court's view, was the admonition that congressionally determined territorial policy should not violate "certain fundamental personal rights declared in the Constitution," a standard not clearly defined by the Court at that time or since.[37]

Thus, from its interpretation in *Downes* that the Foraker Act contained an "implied" policy against U.S. citizenship for the territories acquired from Spain, an interpretation that is a linchpin in the logic of the ruling that Congress did not intend to incorporate these territories, in *Balzac* the Supreme Court takes yet another huge leap into the realm of social and legal policy by declaring that an intention to incorporate cannot be left to "mere inference" based on the conferral of U.S. citizenship in a territory!

As a matter of law and logic the Supreme Court's holding in *Balzac* cannot be reconciled with the Court's previous holding in *Rassmussen,* because, inter alia, the U.S. citizenship conferred on inhabitants of Alaska under the Treaty of Cession from Russia is constitutionally indistinguishable from the citizenship that Congress conferred by statute on residents of Puerto Rico in 1917.[38] Yet, in *Rassmussen,* the Court construed the conferral of citizenship on residents of Alaska as the critical evidence that Congress intended to incorporate Alaska into the Union, while in *Balzac* the Court ruled that the express conferral of U.S. citizenship by Congress on residents of Puerto Rico was not adequate evidence that Congress intended to incorporate Puerto Rico into the Union.[39] In *Balzac* the Supreme Court required a "*declaration of purpose*" by Congress to incorporate the territory, rather than an *inference* based on conferral of citizenship, but in *Rassmussen* the Court *inferred* the intent to incorporate based on conferral of citizenship, even though there was no "*declaration of purpose*" by Congress to do so. The conspicuous deficiencies in this controlling jurisprudence cannot be sustained upon serious scrutiny, yet the destiny of the U.S. citizens of Puerto Rico has been determined for eight decades based on the flawed logic and mind-bending cognitive dissonance of this misconceived ruling.

It is not an overstatement to say that the *Balzac* ruling became a federal judicial mandate for a less-than-equal class of U.S. citizenship for residents of the unincorporated territories. Congressional acquiescence in and eventual statutory confirmation of this judicial policy has left nearly 4 million U.S. citizens in Puerto Rico, as well as the many citizens of smaller island territories (e.g., Guam and the Virgin Islands) without government by consent of the governed or equal rights and duties of national citizenship, or any federally recognized tools of self-determination to end their disenfranchisement.[40]

Although the original *Insular Cases* represented a historically fateful departure from the anticolonial and anti-imperialist tradition of territorial incorporation under the Northwest Ordinance model, the unincorporated territory doctrine invented in those cases expressly applied only to noncitizen territorial populations. In effect, *Balzac* gave Congress a green light to govern U.S. citizens in an unincorporated territory with the same degree of discretion as it governed noncitizen "alien races" under the *Insular Cases*. This placed the U.S. citizens of the unincorporated territories outside the zone of protection and rights under the U.S. Constitution occupied by U.S. citizens in the incorporated territories. In other words, it meant that conferral of U.S. citizenship was legally without consequence, and was not really relevant to the determination of whether a territory was incorporated or unincorporated. Yet, in *Downes* and even more so in *Rassmussen*, the conferral or nonconferral of U.S. citizenship had been the pivotal linchpin criterion for determining whether a territory was incorporated or unincorporated.

This error of logic and irreconcilable legal doctrines is not esoteric; it is material in the most profound respect to what has become an eight-decade denial of government by consent of the governed to a U.S. citizen population that now numbers approximately 4 million. It was *Balzac* that made the unincorporated territory doctrine of the *Insular Cases* applicable even after conferral of U.S. citizenship on residents of U.S. territories, creating the possibility of their indefinite disenfranchisement. U.S. citizens in what the *Insular Cases* declared to be "unincorporated territories" have never been given the rights of citizenship bestowed on U.S. citizens in the incorporated territories during their transition to statehood, and consequently have a citizenship status defined by a federal legal policy that can legally and logically be compared to the reasoning of the *Dred Scott* case.[41]

The Supreme Court's decision in the *Dred Scott* case[42] is infamous for declaring unconstitutional a federal statute limiting the spread of slavery in new territories and states (the so-called Missouri Compromise). The legal effect of the Supreme Court's ruling was to sanction the treatment of those subject to slavery laws as a subclass of human beings whose status and rights were defined and limited by law and social norms. According to the Supreme Court, people brought to America as slaves could not become citizens by living in a free territory or state, in effect putting abolition of slavery through political or legal process out of reach, and thereby setting the stage for the Civil War. It took the Emancipation Proclamation and the Thirteenth, Fourteenth, and Fifteenth Amendments to the U.S. Constitution to undo the effects of the *Dred Scott* case, by ending slavery, granting citizenship to former slaves, and guaranteeing equality to all citizens.

The infamy of the Supreme Court's ruling in the *Dred Scott* case has eclipsed the fact that, to reach its decision, the Supreme Court wrote what should have been a landmark decision in federal territorial law, one that, ironically, the Court failed to follow when it issued its subsequent decisions in *Downes* and *Balzac*. In *Dred Scott*, the Court held that the Constitution applied of its own force in U.S. territories and that territorial residents who were U.S. citizens had rights also enjoyed by citizens in the states of the Union. Thus, while the Supreme Court's decision condemned *Dred Scott* to slavery, and arguably the nation to civil war, the Court's view on territorial law was in the anticolonial tradition of the Northwest Ordinance because it held that U.S. citizens in the territories had rights protected by the Constitution. Perversely, on that basis the Court found that the statute ending slavery in some territories but not others represented an unconstitutional denial of Due Process infringing upon the property rights of U.S. citizen slaveholders migrating to territories that were "free" under the so-called Missouri Compromise.

Unfortunately, in creating and institutionalizing a less-than-equal status for U.S. citizens in the territories acquired from Spain, the Supreme Court's decisions in *Downes* and *Balzac* echoed the worst aspects of the *Dred Scott* decision, but departed from that decision's territorial law holding by not extending to U.S. citizens in "unincorporated" territories protections of the Constitution that the Court had previously applied to uphold the rights of U.S. citizen slaveholders. To the contrary, the majority opinion in *Downes* carefully but explicitly distinguished and departed from the *Dred Scott* decision insofar as it applied the Constitution to U.S. territories,[43] leaving territorial residents in the same unfortunate position that was once shared by slaves and former slaves, Native Americans, and other previously disenfranchised populations who were denied equal rights, or any path to achieve equal rights. In *Balzac*, the U.S. Supreme Court failed to treat Puerto Rico in 1922 the same way it treated Alaska and Hawaii in 1905 and 1903, respectively. The ground rules laid down in the *Mankichi* and *Rassmussen* cases and in the *Insular Cases*, when taken together, were clear. A territory with U.S. citizens is incorporated and subject to the protections of the U.S. Constitution. A territory with a population of nationals but not citizens is unincorporated.

Balzac changed the ground rules for Puerto Rico without the transparency or reconciliation with governing jurisprudence required by judicial responsibility. The result has been the creation of a subclass of U.S. nationality and citizenship for residents of Puerto Rico and for other small unincorporated territories, because Congress accepted the flawed doctrine of *Balzac* without full consideration of the implications.

The Impermanence of Statutory Rights

As the previous discussion of the differences between constitutionally protected citizenship and statutory citizenship illustrate, there are significant differences in consequence between statutory rights granted by Congress in the exercise of its powers under the Territorial Clause and constitutional rights protected by the U.S. Constitution.

Under the Territorial Clause, Congress can apply the U.S. Constitution and any federal treaty or law to the territories. By federal statute, Congress can even agree to restrain itself in the exercise of its territorial powers. U.S. citizens can acquire and enjoy statutory rights under the terms of such statutes while they are in effect. Similarly, federal courts will uphold statutes creating local government structures in the territories as long as the statutes creating those structures remain in effect and unaltered by federal law. However, no Congress can restrict the power of any subsequent Congress to amend or nullify a statute.[44] Thus, any statutory status or rights granted by Congress to a U.S. territory or its residents necessarily lack legal and political permanence because there is no binding future right to a statutory policy.

Notes

[1] The Preamble to the Northwest Ordinance (¶12) contemplated that any statutory form of territorial government would be temporary during incorporation and the transition to statehood. *Act of August 7, 1789*, ch. 8, *Statutes at Large of the United States of America* 1 (1789): 51 n.(a).

[2] Whitney T. Perkins, *Denial of Empire: The United States and Its Dependencies* (Leyden, The Netherlands: A.W. Sythoff, 1962), 14–23. The promise of citizenship did not extend to all persons within our territories, including native tribes and the slave population. See the discussion of the *Dred Scott* decision in the section beginning on page 51 of this chapter.

[3] E.g., *Downes v. Bidwell*, 182 U.S. 244 (1901); *Dorr v. United States*, 195 U.S. 138 (1904).

[4] See *Downes*, 182 U.S. at 287, holding that Puerto Rico, one of the territories acquired from Spain, was "a territory appurtenant and belonging to . . . but not part of the United States within [applicable provisions of] the . . . Constitution."

[5] Ibid.

[6] *Act of April 12, 1900 (Foraker Act)*, ch. 191, *U.S. Statutes at Large* 31 (1900): 77.

[7] *Downes*, 182 U.S. at 280.

[8] Perkins, *Denial of Empire*, 25–26.

[9] See Christina Duffy Burnett and Burke Marshall, eds., *Foreign in a Domestic Sense: Puerto Rico, American Expansion, and the Constitution* (Durham, N.C.: Duke University Press, 2001), 3–4.

[10] Ibid. See, e.g., Christina Duffy Burnett, *United States: American Expansion and Territorial Deannexation*, 72 U. Chi. L. Rev. 797 (2005), which argues that all forms of local government and political status created by Congress under its territorial power are temporary and that the *Insular Cases* served the United States well when they were decided by not allowing the "formal and permanent installation of colonial inequality" to be grafted onto the American political culture in perpetuity, under the guise of "local autonomy" policies that sought to justify and make permanent disenfranchisement tolerable. Ibid., 876.

However, that cogent discussion does not reach the problem of discrimination against residents of territories who have been granted political status as U.S. citizens, which residents of Puerto Rico received in 1917, or the failure of Congress to exercise its authority and responsibility to determine a permanent status policy for Puerto Rico in a deliberate and timely manner.

[11] Justice Brown delivered the opinion of the Court and Justice White and Justice Gray delivered concurring opinions, all consistent with the "imperial-

ist" theory of national sovereignty. Justice Shiras and Justice McKenna joined Justice White's concurring opinion. See Burnett and Marshall, *Foreign in a Domestic Sense*, 5–17.

[12] As recently as 1957, the Supreme Court in effect acknowledged that one basis for the discriminatory doctrine of the *Insular Cases* was ethnic prejudice against the "wholly dissimilar traditions and institutions" of Puerto Rico and the other territories acquired from Spain. *Reid v. Covert*, 354 U.S. 1, 14 (1957). Arguably, Puerto Rico's traditions and institutions were no more "dissimilar" to the rest of the Union than were those of Alaska, California, Hawaii, Louisiana, New Mexico, or Texas when the Constitution was extended to those jurisdictions.

[13] The Court's theory was clearly expressed in the following passage from Justice Brown's opinion:

> If it be once conceded that we are at liberty to acquire foreign territory, a presumption arises that our power with respect to such territories is the same power which other nations have been accustomed to exercise with respect to territories acquired by them. If, in limiting the power which Congress was to exercise within the United States, it was also intended to limit it with regard to such territories . . . such limitations should have been expressed. Instead of that, we find the Constitution speaking only to States, except in the territorial clause, which is absolute in its terms, and suggestive of no limitations upon the power of Congress in dealing with them. The States could only delegate to Congress such powers as they themselves possessed, and as they had no power to acquire new territory they had none to delegate in that connection. The logical inference from this is, that if Congress had power to acquire new territory, which is conceded, that power was not hampered by the constitutional provisions. If, upon the other hand, we assume that the territorial clause of the Constitution was not intended to be restricted to such territory as the United States then possessed, there is nothing in the Constitution to indicate that the power of Congress in dealing with them was intended to be restricted by any of the other provisions.
>
> *Downes*, 182 U.S. at 285–286.

[14] *Act of April 12, 1900 (Foraker Act)*, ch. 191, *U.S. Statutes at Large* 31 (1900): 77.

[15] See *Downes*, 182 U.S. at 279–280.

[16] *Downes*, 182 U.S. at 287. Although *Downes* applied specifically to Puerto Rico, when Congress adopted organic legislation for Guam (*U.S. Code* 48 (2006), § 1421a), it employed the label "unincorporated territory," a term of art from the *Insular Cases*, to describe Guam, making the holding in *Downes* applicable to Guam as well.

[17] The Court's opinion in *Downes* emphasized the "temporary" nature of unincorporated territory status until Congress determined issues of future political status and citizenship. See *Downes*, 182 U.S. at 280, 286–287.

[18] *Rassmussen v. United States*, 197 U.S. 516 (1905); *Hawaii v. Mankichi*, 190 U.S. 197 (1903).

[19] *Rassmussen*, 197 U.S. at 522–523 (emphasis added).

[20] *Mankichi*, 190 U.S. at 209–210; see also *Act of April 30, 1900*, ch. 339, *U.S. Statutes at Large* 31 (1900): 141.

[21] See "Treaty of Peace between the United States of America and the Kingdom of Spain," April 11, 1899, *United States Statutes at Large* 30:1754, Art. IX and section B.4 of this chapter.

[22] *Gonzales v. Williams*, 192 U.S. 1 (1904).

[23] See ibid. at 12–13.

[24] *Lodge Act (Philippine Organic Act)*, Public Law 57-235, *U.S. Statutes at Large* 32 (1902): 691, § 4.

[25] See *Rabang v. Boyd*, 353 U.S. 427 (1957).

[26] See ibid. at 429, citing Section 501 of Title 8 of the U.S. Code.

[27] Persons born in the territory of American Samoa have never been given statutory citizenship but have been classified as nationals. See *U.S. Code* 8 (2006), § 1408, as applicable in light of *U.S. Code* 8 (2006), § 1101(a)(29). A narrow class of persons born in the Northern Mariana Islands—i.e., those born there under special circumstances such as having one alien and one U.S. national parent—are also classified as nationals under *U.S. Code* 8 (2006), § 1408(4), which also cross-references for some purposes Section 1401(g). See *Covenant to Establish a Commonwealth of the Northern Mariana Islands*, Sec. 506(b), Public Law 94-241 (1976), codified at *U.S. Code* 48 (2006), § 1801.

[28] *U.S. Code* 8 (2006), § 1401.

[29] See discussion of *Rogers v. Bellei* in note 47 of chapter 1.

[30] See House Committee on Resources, *Puerto Rico-United States Bilateral Pact of Non-Territorial Permanent Union and Guaranteed Citizenship Act: Hearing on H.R. 4751*, 107th Cong., 1st sess., 2000, Committee Print 107-C (Statement of William M. Treanor, Deputy Assistant Attorney General, Office of Legal Counsel, U.S. Department of Justice; Letter of October 24, 2000, from Dick Thornburgh, former U.S. Attorney General, to Chairman, House Committee on Resources; Letter of November 2, 2000, from Walter E. Dellinger, O'Melveny & Myers, to Chairman, House Committee on Resources).

[31] *Balzac v. Porto Rico*, 258 U.S. 298 (1922).

[32] U.S. citizenship was conferred on persons born in Puerto Rico in 1917. *Act of March 2, 1917 (Jones Act—Puerto Rico)*, ch. 145, *U.S. Statutes at Large* 39 (1917): 951. See section beginning on page 15 of chapter 1.

[33] There is abundant legal literature on the unincorporated territory doctrine of the early *Insular Cases*, as originally applied to noncitizen territorial

populations, the evolution of the incorporation doctrine in *Rassmussen* and *Mankichi,* and the extension of the unincorporated territory doctrine to U.S. citizen populations by Justice Taft in *Balzac.* See, e.g., Burnett and Marshall, *Foreign in a Domestic Sense,* Parts I and II; Bartholomew H. Sparrow, *The Insular Cases and the Emergence of American Empire* (Lawrence: University Press of Kansas, 2006).

34 *Balzac,* 258 U.S. at 304–313.

35 Ibid. at 311. In *The Insular Cases and the Emergence of American Empire* at 201–202, Sparrow reviews Justice Taft's inventory of the features of the 1917 organic act that support a finding of incorporation as well as those supporting a finding of nonincorporation. It seems clear, however, that Justice Taft would accept nothing short of an explicit declaration of incorporation and that his opinion was not grounded in *stare decisis. Rassmussen* and *Mankichi* arguably required a different approach, which was to find for extension of the U.S. Constitution based on conferral of U.S. citizenship and then determine the sufficiency of the jury trial and other provisions in the 1917 organic act on that basis.

36 See *Balzac,* 258 U.S. at 312.

37 See ibid. at 312–313.

38 Naturalization by Congress, whether by treaty or statute, is indistinguishable and does not extend the same Fourteenth Amendment citizenship that arises from birth or naturalization in a state of the Union. Rather, such naturalization measures are promulgated under the Naturalization Clause and enacted as statutory policy at the discretion of Congress for persons who do not acquire citizenship under the Fourteenth Amendment, e.g., for persons born of U.S. parents overseas (*U.S. Code* 8 (2006), § 1401), for persons born in the unincorporated territories (*U.S. Code* 8 (2006), §§ 1402–1407), and for other persons born under U.S. sovereignty and jurisdiction and entitled to the national protection of the United States but outside the reach of the Fourteenth Amendment (*U.S. Code* 8 (2006), § 1408). See *Rogers v. Bellei,* 401 U.S. 815 (1971), in which the Supreme Court held that persons born or naturalized outside the states of the Union have *statutory* citizenship instead of *constitutional* citizenship under the Fourteenth Amendment.

39 See section beginning on page 48 of this chapter.

40 See note 16 of this chapter regarding Guam's status as an "unincorporated territory" under *U.S. Code* 48 (2006), § 1421a. As a result, the reasoning of *Balzac,* which specifically applied only to residents of Puerto Rico, also applies to U.S. citizens in Guam.

41 See Dick Thornburgh, "Dred Scott and Balzac—A Legacy of Equality Denied," *San Juan Star,* July, 14, 2004, 70, which states: "What the Dred Scott and

Balzac cases have in common is that both impose a judicially determined federal policy that people living in a U.S. territory, who have no citizenship other than that of the United States, can be denied full and equal citizenship as well as government by consent of the governed, indefinitely and without legal or political remedy."

[42] The *Dred Scott* case was formally captioned *Scott v. Sandford*, 60 U.S. 393 (1857).

[43] See *Downes*, 182 U.S. at 271–275, and in concurring and dissenting opinions at 291 and 360, respectively.

[44] That is also the conclusion of the U.S. Department of Justice after admitting that it had been inconsistent on the enforceability of "mutual consent" restrictions in the case of the CNMI. See the discussion of the DOJ Memorandum on pages 22–23 of chapter 1. See also discussion on page 30 of chapter 1.

CHAPTER THREE

THE INTERNATIONAL LAW CONTEXT FOR TERRITORIAL STATUS ISSUES

The legal and political context for U.S. treatment of its territories is not necessarily limited to the U.S. Constitution and the legislation enacted by Congress under the Territorial Clause. International law, including the treaties and international covenants the United States has joined, are also important parts of the framework for considering territorial issues, not only as a matter of law but as a matter of international relations and the standing of the United States in the court of worldwide public opinion.

RELEVANT INTERNATIONAL LAW AND INTERNATIONAL AGREEMENTS

For more than 28 years, the United States has been a signatory to the International Covenant on Civil and Political Rights (ICCPR), which states, in Article 1.1: "All peoples have the right of self-determination. By virtue of that right they freely determine their political status and freely pursue their economic, social and cultural development."[1] In Article 25, the ICCPR also states: "Every citizen shall have the right and the opportunity, without . . . unreasonable restrictions: (a) To take part in the conduct of public affairs, directly or through freely chosen representatives; (b) To vote and to be elected at genuine periodic elections which shall be by universal and equal suffrage . . . ."

The United States became a State Party to the ICCPR in 1992. Article 1.3 of the ICCPR requires party governments to "promote the realization of the right of self-determination," and Article 2.1 of the ICCPR provides: "Each State Party to the present Covenant undertakes to respect and to ensure to all individuals within its territory and subject to its jurisdiction the rights recognized in the present Covenant . . . ." Strong arguments can be and have been made that the United States has not met these commitments under the ICCPR with respect to citizens who reside in U.S. territories, such as Puerto Rico.

RELEVANT UNITED NATIONS RESOLUTIONS

The record of UN proceedings relevant to Puerto Rico also remains a source of controversy with regard to compliance by the United States with applicable international agreements and legal standards.

United Nations General Assembly Resolution 748 (VIII),[2] which released the United States from its obligation to report annually on Puerto Rico's progress toward full decolonization and self-government under Article 73(e) of the UN Charter, was approved on November 27, 1953, only hours after the General Assembly also approved Resolution 742 (VIII).[3]

Resolution 742 set forth the criteria for cessation of reporting requirements under Article 73(e) based on attainment of a fully self-governing status. These criteria included "[r]epresentation without discrimination in the central legislative organs" and "[c]itizenship without discrimination . . . on the same basis as other inhabitants." In a 22 to 18 vote approving Resolution 748, with 19 abstentions, the UN General Assembly accepted the result that the United States would no longer report on Puerto Rico, despite the noncompliance of Puerto Rico's status with the criteria established under Resolution 742.[4]

General Assembly Resolution 748 (VIII) states at paragraph 9 that "due regard will be paid to the will of both the Puerto Rican and American peoples in the conduct of their relations under their present legal statute, and also in the eventuality that either of the parties to the mutually agreed association may desire any change in the terms of this association." Thus, Resolution 748 recognizes that Puerto Rico's "commonwealth" status is a creation of federal statute and can be altered in accordance with the U.S. constitutional process, something the United States agreed to do consistent with its domestic and international obligations to respect the principle of self-determination for Puerto Rico.

The results of the 1998 local status vote[5] indicate that the residents of Puerto Rico have withdrawn their consent to be governed under the current "commonwealth" status. The withdrawal of this consent demands serious good faith measures by the federal government to resolve the status of Puerto Rico and to bring the administration of Puerto Rico into compliance with this nation's commitments to the United Nations.

THE FIRST CIRCUIT'S OPINION IN *IGARTÚA*

In 2005 the U.S. Court of Appeals for the First Circuit considered whether U.S. obligations under the ICCPR and other principles of international law were sufficient legal predicates for judicial action to enhance the political rights of the U.S. citizens of Puerto Rico. Although a majority of the First Circuit held that no such judicial action was appropriate in the specific case before it, *Igartúa de la Rosa v. United States*,[6] the very fact that these international law issues were considered by one of the nation's highest courts suggests that judicial intervention to protect the rights of territorial residents may be a future possibility, particularly if Congress continues to defer action on territorial status issues.

The specific issue before the First Circuit in *Igartúa* was whether U.S. citizens in Puerto Rico had a right to vote in U.S. presidential elections. The plaintiffs' efforts to secure that right, on due process and equal protection grounds, had been rejected several times,[7] primarily because the courts had concluded that, under the Electoral College provisions of the Constitution, voting in presidential elections is a function of statehood, and Puerto Rico is not a "state."[8] On March 14, 2005, however, a three-judge panel of the First Circuit granted a petition for rehearing, inviting the parties and others to address "the international legal obligations of the United States with respect to the eligibility of Puerto Rico residents to vote for President and Vice-President of the United States pursuant to international agreements, including . . . the International Covenant on Civil and Political Rights [ICCPR]."[9]

The First Circuit's order granting a rehearing of yet another *Igartúa* appeal held out little promise of specific relief for the aggrieved plaintiffs, who sought to vote in the next U.S. presidential election, but, when coupled with the concurring and dissenting opinions issued in other cases by one of the judges on the First Circuit panel, the order asking for arguments on the effect of international undertakings was significant.[10] For even if the specific measures required for territorial status resolution remain essentially political, the First Circuit was effectively serving notice on Congress and the president that it was taking cognizance of international agreements that might be relevant to the U.S. administration of its territories. Perhaps because of the potential significance of the order granting a rehearing by the three-judge panel, the rehearing in *Igartúa* was converted to an en banc review after the parties and several *amici curiae* (friends of the court) had filed briefs in the case.[11]

On August 3, 2005, the First Circuit issued its ruling on the petition for rehearing en banc.[12] Predictably, a majority of the First Circuit rejected plaintiff Igartúa's claim that, under international law, U.S. citizens of Puerto Rico have a legal right to vote in presidential elections, noting that, in light of the specific language of the Electoral College provisions of the Constitution, Puerto Rico would have to become a state or the Constitution would need to be amended before U.S. citizens in Puerto Rico would be entitled to vote for the electors who choose a president after a national election.[13]

The majority also rejected the arguments made by both Igartúa and certain *amici* that the courts should issue some form of declaratory relief to enforce U.S. treaty commitments—e.g., under the ICCPR—to ensure universal suffrage on the ground that provisions of the ICCPR were not self-executing.[14]

Circuit Judge Torruella and Circuit Judge Howard both wrote strong dissenting opinions that strenuously rebutted the majority's opinion.[15] Judge Torruella in particular reinforced his concern that U.S. leadership in the region and in the international community would be encumbered by the failure to practice in our own territory what we espouse to the world, particularly since those principles are embodied in international agreements and conventions to which the United States is a party.[16]

The dissenting judges did not limit themselves to a discussion of the international law implications of Puerto Rico's status, but took direct aim at Supreme Court precedents that have contributed to the less-than-equal status of U.S. citizens in Puerto Rico. For instance, Judge Torruella characterized the Supreme Court's decision in *Balzac v. Porto Rico* as an incorrect application of the earlier *Insular Cases*.[17] Judge Torruella also made an argument that had not been fully developed by judges in the past—that is, the Supreme Court's opinion in *Balzac* is incompatible with its previous decision in *Rassmussen v. United States*.[18] Judge Torruella's dissent concluded that, in light of the problems created by the *Balzac* decision, it is time for the Supreme Court to reconsider and overrule that decision.[19]

Judge Torruella also criticized Congress for taking so long to resolve the political status of Puerto Rico, pointing out that Puerto Rico's territorial status was intended to be temporary.[20] Judge Torruella observed that, almost 50 years ago, in *Reid v. Covert*,[21] when the Supreme Court defined and gave effect to the "fundamental rights" of U.S. citizens who reside in England, the Court rationalized its rulings in the *Insular Cases* and in *Balzac*, which had denied the rights of full citizenship to residents and U.S. citizens of Puerto Rico, by stating that those territorial cases "involved the power of Congress to provide rules and regulations to govern *temporarily* territories with wholly dissimilar traditions and institutions . . . ."[22] Judge Torruella suggested that the ethnic prejudice these opinions revealed and the long delay by Congress in ensuring full civil rights for the residents of Puerto Rico represent violations of the Fifth Amendment's guarantees of due process and equal protection.[23] It is hard not to agree with Judge Torruella's analysis. In this author's view, a territorial status that has lasted more than 100 years since the Treaty of Peace with Spain—almost 90 years since Congress bestowed partial and temporary citizenship on residents of Puerto Rico and more than 50 years since Puerto Rico adopted a local constitution—cannot reasonably be characterized as a "temporary" status that justifies a denial of full rights to self-determination and self-governance.

Finally, Judge Torruella attacked the majority in *Igartúa* for pretending that status resolution for Puerto Rico is a purely political question and that the residents of Puerto Rico merely need to summon the political will to decide whether to seek independence or statehood.[24] Judge Torruella also attacked the majority's incorrect description of Puerto Rico's present "commonwealth" structure of local self-government as a unique political "status" that significantly redeems principles of self-determination, when in fact Puerto Rico's "commonwealth" government is not an adequate alternative to statehood or independence because it merely implements limited local civil government at the discretion of Congress and does not provide citizens in Puerto Rico with a right to self-government at a national level.[25]

Although the First Circuit denied the specific relief sought in the *Igartúa* case, the arguments and sharply divided opinions in that case focused the attention of one of the nation's highest courts on several issues that cannot be ignored.

First, more than 100 years after the U.S. commitment in the 1898 Treaty of Peace with Spain that Congress would determine the "civil rights and political status" of the residents of Puerto Rico and other former Spanish colonies,[26] Congress still has not decided the ultimate political status of Puerto Rico or developed a procedure that would entitle the residents of Puerto Rico to full self-government based on equal rights of national citizenship.

Second, as the Supreme Court recognized in the *Insular Cases*, the territorial status that Puerto Rico now holds was never intended to be more than temporary. Although the Supreme Court's decision in *Balzac* and the "commonwealth" form of local self-government adopted by Puerto Rico in accordance with Public Law 600[27] may have confused the issue, there is no good reason why Congress, in the more than eight decades since the *Balzac* decision in 1922 and in the more than five decades since the adoption of the Puerto Rican constitution in 1952, has not exercised its power and responsibility under the Territorial Clause to determine whether Puerto Rico should become another state of the Union (like Alaska and Hawaii did in 1959) or an independent nation (like the Philippines became in 1946). The political limbo in which Puerto Rico has existed for more than 100 years is not required by or consistent with the Constitution, the Treaty of Peace with Spain, this nation's historic treatment of territories, or relevant Supreme Court precedent.

Third, the less-than-equal citizenship of residents of Puerto Rico is not consistent with the international commitments the United States has made, in the ICCPR and elsewhere, to ensure democracy, self-determination, and universal and equal suffrage for all persons under its jurisdiction.

Fourth, as a matter of foreign policy and international world opinion, it is difficult, if not impossible, to reconcile the many statements made by U.S. leaders in support of democracy and self-determined freedom elsewhere around the world with a system of government that prevents residents of Puerto Rico, upon whom Congress conferred citizenship status in 1917,[28] from voting for national leaders, from electing full members of the Congress that determines the federal laws to which they are subject, and from even deciding their ultimate status among legally valid status options recognized by Congress.

The ultimate message of *Igartúa* may be that a time will come when the federal courts, even the Supreme Court, will no longer be complacent if Congress fails to deal with the political status of Puerto Rico and the rights of its citizens to self-determination and self-government at a national level. When that time comes, judicial action is likely to take the form of declaratory relief.

THE POWER OF THE COURTS TO ISSUE DECLARATORY RELIEF

Federal courts have long recognized that it is the function of the courts "to finally and authoritatively interpret what the law says."[29] The Declaratory Judgment Act provides the courts with the option of "declar[ing] the rights and other legal relations of any interested party seeking such declaration, whether or not further relief is or could be sought."[30] One of the principal criteria in favor of rendering a declaratory judgment is "when the judgment will serve a useful purpose in clarifying and settling the legal relations in issue."[31]

The courts have recognized that declaratory relief is an appropriate mechanism for "clarifying and settling the legal relations" between the United States and the inhabitants of territories under federal administration pursuant to both U.S. and international law.[32] "It is the role of the judiciary to interpret international treaties and to enforce domestic rights arising from them."[33] Thus, although the First Circuit denied the declaratory relief sought by the plaintiff in *Igartúa*, the power of the courts to issue declaratory relief to territorial residents is itself not in doubt.

Even judicial action short of a declaratory judgment can be important in defining territorial rights. In *Juda v. United States*,[34] the U.S. Claims Court used its power to interpret international agreements as a way of persuading the political branches of government to take action consistent with those agreements. The issue in *Juda* was whether, as a matter of international law, the United States could unilaterally terminate its trusteeship over the Marshall Islands and other Pacific island territories without securing the approval of the UN Security Council.[35] The Claims Court stated that "[c]ourts of the United States have final authority to interpret an international agreement for purposes of applying it as law in the United States."[36]

The Claims Court held that actions by the president and Congress to resolve the status of the Pacific Island Trust Territories had resulted in *de facto* but not *de jure* compliance by the United States with its treaty obligations.[37] Because of its hortatory impact, this ruling provided a form of declaratory relief to trust territory citizens who had challenged the validity under international law of the declaration in Proclamation 5564[38] that the trusteeship was no longer in effect. Although the Claims Court denied the specific relief sought by the trust territory citizens on other grounds, it did agree with their argument that Proclamation 5564 was not in compliance with applicable treaties, including the UN Charter. In the view of the Claims Court, although the president, by issuing Proclamation 5564, could recognize a new political status for the Republic of the Marshall Islands under a Compact of Free Association as a matter of *de facto* domestic law, the Claims Court withheld *de jure* recognition of the proclamation's validity, which, the Claims Court said, would not be possible until the government took appropriate steps to meet U.S. obligations under the UN Charter.[39]

The government did in fact take such steps by seeking and obtaining, along with each of four new governments emerging from the Trust Territories, UN Security Council approval of Resolution 956 on November 10, 1994. Although the Claims Court did not retain jurisdiction during the seven-year period until the Security Council adopted Resolution 956, the government faithfully followed the road map the Claims Court had provided and did conform the status resolution process for the Trust Territories to the *de jure* principles articulated in the Claims Court's *Juda* decision. At that point, *de facto* domestic law and *de jure* international law converged.

The outcome in *Juda* suggests that federal courts need not simply defer to the political branches of government when faced with issues regarding territorial administration but that they can play a useful role, even while respecting separation of powers principles, in outlining the path to be taken by the political branches of government to resolve the political status of U.S. territories and to comply with international agreements that affect the rights of people who reside in those territories. For precisely that reason, Circuit Judge Torruella cited *Juda* in his dissenting opinion in *Igartúa* in support of his argument that the federal courts can and should play a more active role in achieving status resolution for Puerto Rico.[40]

In concurring with the majority in *Igartúa*, Circuit Judge Lipez rejected Judge Torruella's analysis of *Juda* by arguing, in this author's view incorrectly, that U.S. noncompliance with treaty obligations in that case had been "due to a technical misunderstanding" and that the corrective actions taken by the U.S. government had been "a near certainty" all along.[41] Judge Lipez's characterization is not supported by the record in the case. The order of the Court in the case reflects that the issue of compliance with international law, the UN Charter and the Trusteeship Agreement was a substantive and material issue vigorously contested by the parties. That it was also the subject of internal debate within the U.S. government and in diplomatic efforts related to proceedings of the UN Trusteeship Council and Security Council when the trusteeship termination question came before them is reflected in the somewhat unprecedented language adopted by Congress in approving the legislation to end the U.S. trusteeship over the Pacific island territories. Recognizing an element of uncertainty and the substantive, rather than technical, nature of the treaty issues in question, Congress provided that the new Compact of Free Association with the Marshall Islands not take effect until the United States had "taken into account any procedures with respect to the United Nations for termination of the Trusteeship Agreement."[42] Instead of simply approving the compact, Congress explicitly recognized satisfaction of UN procedures in the UN Security Council and Trusteeship Council. Thus, Circuit Judge Lipez's critique of *Juda*, which remains an important example of how the federal courts can play a constructive role in resolving territorial status issues, attempts to minimize and oversimplify what the Court and Congress recognized as a material legal and diplomatic question.

Furthermore, in *Juda*, the Claims Court rejected the U.S. argument that the *Insular Cases* precluded extension of constitutional rights to the U.S.-administered Trust Territory of the Pacific Islands.[43] Instead, the Claims Court ruled that, even in a territory with a noncitizen population governed under a treaty with the United Nations instead of as a result of annexation, "[a]ll of the restraints of the Bill of Rights are applicable to the United States wherever it has acted. The concept that the Bill of Rights and other constitutional protections against arbitrary government are to be applied selectively on a territorial basis cannot be justified in the 1980's."[44] It is now 2006 and Puerto Rico is still waiting for Congress to recognize that nine decades of U.S. citizenship requires a higher standard of rights than those available to noncitizens in the territories under the *Insular Cases*.

Notes

[1] The ICCPR was opened for signature on December 16, 1966, 999 U.N.T.S. 171. The United States became a signatory party on October 5, 1977, and a ratifying full State Party on June 8, 1992. The Universal Declaration of Human Rights

(UDHR), G.A. res. 217A (III), UN Doc A/810 (1948), is the original source of these principles in the ICCPR. See Clause 3 to the Preamble to the ICCPR. For example, Article 25 of the ICCPR adopts the standards of "universal and equal" suffrage adopted by the United Nations in Article 21(3) of the UDHR, which states, "The will of the people . . . shall be expressed in periodic and genuine elections which shall be by universal and equal suffrage . . . ."

[2] G.A. Res. 748, U.N. GAOR, 8th sess., Supp. No. 17, U.N. Doc A/2630 (1953).

[3] G.A. Res. 742, U.N. GAOR, 8th sess., Supp. No. 17, U.N. Doc A/2630 (1953). See House Committee on Resources, *Report on United States–Puerto Rico Political Status Act*, prepared by Mr. Young of Alaska, 104th Cong., 2d sess., 1996, H. Rep. 104-713, Part 1, 13–14; House Committee on Resources, *Report on United States–Puerto Rico Political Status Act*, prepared by Mr. Young of Alaska, 105th Cong., 1st sess., 1997, H. Rep. 105-131, Part 1, 16–17.

[4] House Report 104-713, Part 1, 12.

[5] See discussion on page 20 of chapter 1.

[6] *Igartúa de la Rosa v. United States*, 417 F.3d 145 (1st Cir. 2005), *cert. denied*, 126 S. Ct. 1569 (2006).

[7] *Igartúa de la Rosa v. United States*, 32 F.3d 8 (1st Cir. 1994), *cert. denied*, 514 U.S. 1049 (1995) ("*Igartúa I*"); *Igartúa de la Rosa v. United States*, 229 F.3d 80 (1st Cir. 2000) ("*Igartúa II*"); *Igartúa de la Rosa v. United States*, 386 F.3d 313 (1st Cir. 2004) ("*Igartúa III*").

[8] *Igartúa I*, 32 F.3d at 9–10; *Igartúa II*, 229 F.3d at 83–84. The U.S. Court of Appeals for the Ninth Circuit reached a similar conclusion with respect to the voting rights of U.S. citizens in Guam. *U.S. Citizens Residing in Guam v. United States*, 738 F.2d 1017 (9th Cir. 1984), *cert. denied*, 469 U.S. 1209 (1985).

[9] *Igartúa de la Rosa v. United States*, 404 F.3d 1 (1st Cir. 2005).

[10] *See* the concurring opinion of Circuit Judge Torruella in *Igartúa II*, 229 F.3d at 85-90, and the dissenting opinion of Judge Torruella in *Igartúa III*, 386 F.3d at 314–320.

[11] *Igartúa de la Rosa v. United States*, 407 F.3d 30 (1st Cir. 2005).

[12] *Igartúa de la Rosa v. United States*, 417 F.3d 145 (1st Cir. 2005).

[13] Ibid. at 147–149.

[14] Ibid. at 149–151. The U.S. Declaration of June 8, 1992, that the ICCPR's provisions are not "self-executing" does not excuse the United States from its obligation as a party to the ICCPR for good-faith, affirmative steps to "ensure" rights recognized under the ICCPR. As argued at length below, *de facto* non-compliance under domestic law does not release a party to a treaty from the *de*

jure obligations of that treaty. See discussion of *Juda v. United States*, 13 Cl. Ct. 667 (1987), in the section beginning on page 67 of this chapter.

[15] *Igartúa*, 417 F.3d at 158–184 and 184–192, respectively.

[16] Ibid. at 170–179.

[17] Ibid. at 166–169.

[18] Ibid. at 165–167. See page 52 of chapter 2 for discussion of the contradictions between *Balzac* and *Rassmussen*.

[19] *Igartúa*, 417 F.3d at 169.

[20] Ibid. at 167–168.

[21] *Reid v. Covert*, 354 U.S. 1 (1957).

[22] Ibid. at 14 (emphasis added); *Igartúa*, 417 F.3d at 167. See the discussion of *Reid* in Judge Torruella's concurring opinion in *Igartúa II* at n.14.

[23] *Igartúa*, 417 F.3d at 169–170.

[24] Ibid. at 168.

[25] Ibid. at n. 21.

[26] See "Treaty of Peace between the United States of America and the Kingdom of Spain," April 11, 1899, *United States Statutes at Large* 30:1754.

[27] See pages 16–17 of chapter 1 for a discussion of Public Law 600.

[28] *Act of March 2, 1917 (Jones Act—Puerto Rico)*, ch. 145, *U.S. Statutes at Large* 39 (1917): 951.

[29] Norman J. Singer, *Sutherland Statutory Construction*, 6th ed., vol. 2A (West Group, 2000), § 45:03.

[30] *U.S. Code* 28 (2006), § 2201(a).

[31] *Aetna Casualty & Surety Co. v. Quarles*, 92 F.2d 321, 325 (4th Cir. 1937).

[32] See the dissenting opinion of Judge Torruella in *Igartúa*, 417 F.3d at 180.

[33] *United States v. Decker*, 600 F.2d 733, 737 (9th Cir. 1979).

[34] *Juda v. United States*, 13 Cl. Ct. 667 (1987) ("*Juda II*"). See also *Juda v. United States*, 6 Cl. Ct. 441 (1984) ("*Juda I*").

[35] See section beginning on page 27 of chapter 1 for a discussion of the U.S. role as a UN Trustee over the Trust Territory of the Pacific Islands.

[36] *Juda II*, 13 Cl. Ct. at 678.

[37] Ibid. at 682.

[38] President, Proclamation, "Proclamation 5564," sec. 1, *Federal Register* 51 (November 1986): 40399. See note 157 in chapter 1.

[39] *Juda II*, 13 Cl. Ct. at 678–682.

[40] *Igartúa*, 417 F.3d at 181.

[41] Ibid. at 157.

[42] *Compact of Free Association Act of 1985*, Public Law 99-239, *U.S. Statutes at Large* 99 (1986): 1773, § 101(b).

[43] *Juda I*, 6 Cl. Ct. 441, 458 (1984).

[44] Ibid.

CHAPTER FOUR

EXECUTIVE BRANCH EFFORTS TO RESOLVE THE POLITICAL STATUS OF PUERTO RICO

Although only Congress has the authority to resolve the political status of Puerto Rico and other U.S. territories, the executive branch has tried to encourage congressional action by offering its advice and constitutional analysis[1] and by promulgating instruments of executive branch policy regarding self-determination, status options, and development of self-government in the territories. The most recent and most important such effort by the executive branch was the report issued in December 2005 by the President's Task Force on Puerto Rico's Status.

The origins of that report can be traced at least as far back as November 30, 1992, when then president George H.W. Bush issued a memorandum (the "Bush Memo") calling for referenda within Puerto Rico regarding the island's political status: "As long as Puerto Rico is a territory . . . the will of its people regarding their political status should be ascertained periodically by means of a general right of referendum or specific referenda sponsored either by the United States Government or the Legislature of Puerto Rico." [2] After the 1992 Bush Memo, locally sponsored status votes conducted in Puerto Rico in November 1993 and December 1998 were inconclusive, arguably because of confusion and ambiguity among voters over what legally valid and politically realistic status options were available to Puerto Rico.[3]

This led to promulgation of an executive order by President Clinton on December 23, 2000,[4] establishing the President's Task Force on Puerto Rico's Status ("President's Task Force"), a White House task force to help clarify "options for Puerto Rico's future status that are not incompatible with the Constitution and basic laws and policies of the United States." On December 3, 2003, President George W. Bush signed another executive order,[5] amending the executive order issued by President Clinton, which required the President's Task Force to issue a report on Puerto Rico's status options and procedures to achieve status resolution before the end of 2005. At the same time, President Bush appointed members of the President's Task Force from each federal agency with an interest in the subject and named officials from the White House Intergovernmental Affairs Staff and the Department of Justice as its cochairs.

On December 22, 2005, the White House released the report of the President's Task Force to the public.[6] That report is a long overdue but very important and broadly welcomed effort to address the issues of territorial law and policy that relate to Puerto Rico. The President's Task Force recognized that "the authority under the U.S. Constitution to establish a permanent non-territorial status for the Commonwealth of Puerto Rico rests with Congress."[7] To help set the agenda for congressional consideration of Puerto Rico's status issues, the report offered the following advice regarding the options available to Congress under the U.S. Constitution:

- "The U.S. Constitution allows for three options for the future status of Puerto Rico: continuing territorial status (including the current Commonwealth system), statehood, and independence."[8]
- Statehood and independence are the "only two non-territorial options recognized by the U.S. Constitution that establish a permanent status between the people of Puerto Rico and the Government of the United States."[9]
- "Free association" is a treaty-based bilateral relationship between two nations consistent with independence, and that option is closest to proposals in Puerto Rico to give the present "commonwealth" system for territorial government a more autonomous and nonterritorial status, but Congress would have to agree to all features of the treaty, and under free association or independence there are legal and policy reasons why Congress would not continue the current statutory policy of granting U.S. citizenship in Puerto Rico.[10]

On the basis of these findings, the President's Task Force made the following recommendations:

- Within a year, Congress should provide for federal sponsorship and recognition of a self-determination process in Puerto Rico, including a plebiscite on a date certain, so voters in Puerto Rico can express a preference to either remain a territory or seek a "Constitutionally viable path toward a permanent non-territorial status."[11]

- If voters in Puerto Rico elect to seek a permanent nonterritorial status, Congress should sponsor a plebiscite on the statehood and independence options, including free association terminable by either party; thereafter, Congress should prescribe terms for transition to the option chosen in the second plebiscite.[12]
- If voters in Puerto Rico choose to retain territory status, periodic plebiscites should be conducted to ensure that the form of government in Puerto Rico is based on consent of the governed.[13]

The President's Task Force report represents a significant initiative at the highest levels of the executive branch to establish a set of principles and policies for the resolution of Puerto Rico's political status. The fact that the President's Task Force and its report represent the result of a sustained bipartisan effort by three successive presidential administrations should give its recommendations added weight and credibility before Congress. Although some local politicians in Puerto Rico may favor other status options—including a so-called enhanced commonwealth formula for a new status that does not exist under current U.S. laws[14]—the President's Task Force report has clearly established a standard of compatibility with the U.S. Constitution that any status resolution proposal will have to satisfy to be taken seriously.

Notes

[1] One example of such advice is the 1994 DOJ Memorandum discussed in the section beginning on page 21 of chapter 1.

[2] President, Memorandum, "Memorandum of November 30, 1992," *Federal Register* 57 (December 1992): 57093.

[3] See section beginning on page 15 of chapter 1.

[4] Executive Order no. 13,183, *Federal Register* 65 (December 2000): 251.

[5] Executive Order no. 13,319, *Federal Register* 68 (December 2003): 235.

[6] President's Task Force on Puerto Rico's Status, *Report by the President's Task Force on Puerto Rico's Status* (December 2005), available at http://www.house.gov/fortuno/pdf/PuertoRicoBooklet.pdf.

[7] Ibid., 10.

[8] Ibid., 5.

[9] Ibid., 10.

[10] Ibid., 8–9. Federal statutes and treaties with the force and effect of federal law recognize that independence and treaty-based "free association," terminable at will by either party, consistent with the right of independence, are legitimate status resolution options for territories under U.S. administration

and subject to the Territorial Clause power of Congress. See G.A. Res. 1541, U.N. GAOR, 15th sess., Supp. No. 16, U.N. Doc. A/4684 (1960); G.A. Res. 2625, U.N. GAOR, 25th sess., Supp. No. 28, U.N. Doc. A/8082 (1970). See also *Compact of Free Association Act of 1985*, Public Law 99-239, *U.S. Statutes at Large* 99 (1986): 1770 (US-Marshall Islands-Micronesia); *Compact of Free Association between the United States and Palau*, Public Law 99-658, *U.S. Statutes at Large* 100 (1986): 3672; *Compact of Free Association between the United States and Palau*, Public Law 101-219, *U.S. Statutes at Large* 103 (1989): 1870.

[11] *Report by the President's Task Force on Puerto Rico's Status*, 10.

[12] Ibid.

[13] Ibid.

[14] See chapter 5.

CHAPTER FIVE

INHERENT PROBLEMS WITH "ENHANCED COMMONWEALTH" PROPOSALS

Because Congress has not sponsored sustained, concerted, and conclusive self-determination or status resolution processes for the unincorporated territories, some local government officials have shifted their focus away from historically and legally normative status options, such as statehood or independence, that would provide full government by consent. Instead, to fill the vacuum created by inaction at the federal level, local leaders looking for a way out of the colonial dilemma of unincorporated territory status have devoted decades of effort advocating hybrid status alternatives that purport to combine features of incorporated and unincorporated territory status, as well as implausible combinations of permanent political union with political independence. The inventors and authors of these experimental status theories seek to define a "third path" that makes the difficult choice between statehood and independence unnecessary. Instead of recognizing that statehood and territorial status are the only two options available as long as the U.S. flag flies over a territory and that independence with or without a treaty of free association are the only two options for a nonterritory status, an ideology focused on "autonomy" and "indigenous nationhood" has emerged in some unincorporated territories based on proposals to convert "commonwealth" status into a new hybrid status alternative that has never existed in the territories.

A common mistake associated with these proposals is that they attribute too much significance to a territory's description as a "commonwealth," which is a word used in the names of various types of political entities. For example, the term "commonwealth" is used in the names of four states (including the author's home state of Pennsylvania) without any suggestion that such states have a different political status from other states not designated by the term "commonwealth."

The pattern and common element of proposals for new so-called enhanced commonwealth status options is to take the autonomy features of the Philippines pre-independence commonwealth model and some features of separate sovereignty under the Micronesian free association model and combine those with features of territorial status and/or statehood, such as U.S. nationality and citizenship, open migration to the United States, federal economic subsidies, and permanent union with the United States.

Advocates of such "enhanced commonwealth" proposals have misplaced their reliance on the Philippines model of "commonwealth" government and other features of actual separate nationhood. Among other things, the "commonwealth" structure Congress approved for the Philippines was explicitly intended to ready that territory for independence outside the U.S. constitutional system, whereas the "commonwealth" structures proposed for Guam and adopted for Puerto Rico and the CNMI were intended to provide their local governments with limited powers to oversee local affairs until federally sponsored self-determination processes led to adoption of a federal policy leading to their incorporation and eventual statehood, or to their sovereignty as separate nations.[1]

Nevertheless, over a period of years, local government officials from the Northern Mariana Islands, Guam, and Puerto Rico have pushed, prodded, and pleaded with Congress to grant them more autonomy over local affairs and even some international affairs.[2] At the same time, these "autonomists" have asked Congress to adopt the "unalterable compact" and "mutual consent" features of the Northwest Ordinance model of incorporation so that the statutory rights and privileges of territorial residents, including their rights to U.S. citizenship, and the limited local autonomy of territorial governments could not be changed without local consent. From the perspective of many of these autonomists, a statutory political union with the United States that could not be changed without "mutual consent" would be an adequate substitute for full government by consent and equal rights of national citizenship.

NORTHERN MARIANA ISLANDS

During the Cold War era, Congress found policy experiments in territorial autonomy more practical and convenient than addressing the underlying issue of status resolution. The so-called commonwealth model

Congress adopted to bring the Northern Mariana Islands under U.S. sovereignty in 1976 was the closest Congress ever came to agreeing to a form of local self-government that could not be altered without mutual consent.[3]

However, the legislative history of congressional ratification of the CNMI arrangement, its judicial interpretation by the federal courts, and the DOJ Memorandum (regarding the Guam Commonwealth Act) all support the view that a "mutual consent" provision, embodying a statutory policy of Congress to refrain from exercising its full powers under the Territorial Clause, would not be binding on a future Congress.[4]

GUAM

The DOJ Memorandum caused the Interior Department to formally oppose the Guam Commonwealth Act that Guam's nonvoting delegate first introduced in Congress in 1987 and reintroduced in every subsequent Congress for 10 years.[5] That legislative proposal, and the debate leading to its failure before Congress in 1997, demonstrated the confusion, the legal contradictions, and the political controversy that have led to the disarray in federal territorial policy over the past 100 years.

The Guam Commonwealth Act had been touted by Guam's leaders as the means to secure territorial self-government against incursions by Congress in ways that would redeem principles of autonomy and government by consent. They sought a federal-territorial relationship that had features of separate sovereignty and permanent political union with the United States under federal law. Instead of following the Northwest Ordinance model of incorporation as a state or the Philippines model of autonomy leading to independence as a sovereign nation, Guam sought to combine features of those two models with the free association concept to which the United States had agreed for the Pacific Island Trust Territories after they became sovereign and independent nations[6] and to make those arrangements permanent and binding on Congress under a legal framework that could not be changed without the consent of Guam.

Guam's negotiators tried to premise the Guam Commonwealth Act on other relationships to which the United States had agreed and even proposed that Congress might be able to bind itself or cede its Territorial Clause powers. The Justice Department clarified its position on mutual consent in 1994, however, making it impossible for Interior Department officials to be coy or indirect any longer about the federal government's position on such a commonwealth status and sounding the death knell for the Guam Commonwealth Act, as proposed at that time, when Interior Department representatives testified before the House Committee on Resources on October 29, 1997.[7]

PUERTO RICO

The Guam Commonwealth Act was derived in part from the ideology and platform of the Puerto Rican political party that has also sought a hybrid political status for Puerto Rico. The difference between the "commonwealth" structure proposed in the Guam Commonwealth Act and the Puerto Rican pro-commonwealth party's so-called enhanced commonwealth proposal is that Guam's proposal was compatible with the "commonwealth" structure Congress granted to the Northern Mariana Islands in 1976, which was recognized and accepted as a statutory political union established by Congress in the exercise of its powers under the Territorial Clause.[8] The "enhanced commonwealth" proposal advocated by the pro-commonwealth party in Puerto Rico is a more aggressively separatist ideology.[9] The autonomists in Puerto Rico contend that Congress can and should authorize a new nonterritorial status with Puerto Rico that is unalterable without local consent and no longer subject to the Territorial Clause powers of Congress or the *Insular Cases* doctrine.[10]

Under their proposal for an "enhanced commonwealth" for Puerto Rico, the United States would recognize Puerto Rico as a separate sovereign nation with its own foreign relations powers. It would enter into permanent political union with the sovereign nation-state of Puerto Rico, but allow residents of Puerto Rico to maintain their U.S. citizenship while guaranteeing that these arrangements would remain in existence in perpetuity.[11] Although the Puerto Rican advocates of such an "enhanced commonwealth" structure have invoked the terminology (but not the legal reality) of a "free association" between the United States and Puerto Rico, the "free association" they favor would be much different from the Compact of Free Association that the United States made with the Pacific island territories. As accepted by Congress in the case of Micronesia, Palau, and the Marshall Islands, free association remains terminable at will by the United States and the associated republic, so that it can be recognized juridically as nonterritorial and noncolonial. Furthermore, the Compact of Free Association did not extend U.S. nationality or any form of statutory citizenship to residents of the associated island states. Although residents of the associated states have had a visa waiver that allows them to enter the United States for some purposes, that right has been subject to restrictions that have grown more limiting over the years.[12] Those rights do not compare with the rights that residents of Puerto Rico now have as U.S. citizens to travel to the United States without restriction.

Contrary to the assumptions of the autonomists in Puerto Rico, "free association" is an international status model for decolonization of dependent territories that are not ready for full independence and can be implemented under the U.S. constitutional system only between separate sovereign nations, not as part of a political union that provides core benefits often associated with unincorporated territory status—including U.S. nationality and citizenship.

Of course, a so-called commonwealth system of limited local self-government as authorized by Congress for an unincorporated territory, including a locally adopted constitution, can be "developed," "improved," or "enhanced" by federal and local law consistent with federal territorial law and policy. What is not legally possible or politically realistic is to indefinitely delay status resolution based on options that combine features of incorporation and statehood with features of free association and independence, in an "enhanced commonwealth" proposal that is on its face incompatible with the Constitution, laws, and policies of the United States.

Notes

[1] See sections beginning on pages 12, 15, 21, and 28 of chapter 1.

[2] Local officials from the Virgin Islands and American Samoa have not joined these requests because of the idiosyncrasies of their internal political development.

[3] See section beginning on page 28 of chapter 1.

[4] See sections beginning on pages 21 and 28 of chapter 1 and the section beginning on page 55 of chapter 2.

[5] See section beginning on page 21 of chapter 1.

[6] The Guam commonwealth proposal was influenced in part by the terms under which the United States had terminated its UN trusteeship and administration

of the nearby islands of Micronesia, the Marshall Islands, and Palau. Under a Compact of Free Association, the United States continued close political relations and provided substantial assistance to these new nations based in many respects on the territorial model for island area development. *Compact of Free Association Act of 1985*, Public Law 99-239, *U.S. Statutes at Large* 99 (1986): 1770. See section beginning on page 27 of chapter 1.

[7] See discussion of Deputy Secretary Garamendi's testimony on page 23 of chapter 1.

[8] See *Covenant to Establish a Commonwealth of the Northern Mariana Islands*, Public Law 94-241 (1976), codified at *U.S. Code* 48 (2006), § 1801.

[9] See *Puerto Rico–United States Bilateral Pact of Non-territorial Permanent Union and Guaranteed Citizenship Act*, HR 4751, 106th Cong., 2d sess. (June 26, 2000).

[10] See H.R. 4751, § 2.

[11] Ibid.

[12] *Compact of Free Association Amendments Act of 2003*, sec. 141, Public Law 108-188, *U.S. Statutes at Large* 117 (2003): 2760–2764.

CHAPTER SIX

RECOMMENDED COURSES OF ACTION BY CONGRESS AND THE COURTS

As this volume's historical and legal analysis of political status issues reveals, both Congress and the local territorial governments continue to struggle, in varying degrees, with the challenge of reconciling unincorporated territory status with the principles of American constitutional democracy, including the fundamental right of U.S. citizens to government by consent of the governed.

For almost all U.S. citizens, government by consent has been implemented under the U.S. Constitution, through the federal political system, through representation in Congress, and through participation in national presidential elections. But those rights have not been extended to residents of U.S. territories, even to territorial residents who have been granted U.S. citizenship. To rationalize this unprecedented policy of indefinite territorial status in the twentieth century, Congress accepted and codified the judicially created doctrine of unincorporated territory status developed by the U.S. Supreme Court in the *Insular Cases*.[1]

The acquisition of large, populated territories that Congress did not seek to incorporate under the anticolonial traditions of the Northwest Ordinance required a new territorial policy. When Congress faltered in adopting measures for governance of the new territories acquired from Spain at the end of the nineteenth century, the Supreme Court stepped in and filled the void by creating a legal policy for the administration of those territories that reflected a sharp departure from our nation's past customs and traditions. As noted above, the *Insular Cases* doctrine originally applied only to territories inhabited by noncitizen aliens who were under the national protection of the United States. The Supreme Court's decisions to place such peoples outside the protections of the

U.S. Constitution could be rationalized on the basis that they were not U.S. citizens.

Unfortunately, the Supreme Court's 1922 decision in *Balzac v. Porto Rico*[2] extended the discriminatory impact of the *Insular Cases* doctrine by denying application of the U.S. Constitution to the residents of Puerto Rico even after Congress granted them U.S. citizenship in 1917. As a result, *Balzac* became an unfortunate legal justification for organizing unincorporated territorial governments that lacked sovereign powers beyond those derived from federal statutory authorizations, while simultaneously granting U.S. citizenship to the residents of those territories without providing them with any means to redeem the fundamental right of government by consent at the national level. In this manner, *Balzac* introduced the central constitutional contradiction of unincorporated territory status for all territories with U.S. citizen populations.

The response of Congress to the "judicial activism" embodied in the *Insular Cases* and *Balzac* has been to adopt measures permitting government by consent of the governed only at the local level, without addressing the fact that these U.S. citizens are disenfranchised in the nation of their citizenship, or considering whether government by consent of the governed is a fundamental right of U.S. citizens under the U.S. Constitution. The congressional policy of limited local self-government for unincorporated territories began with organic acts that authorized local government by federal appointees, then by local legislative bodies, and finally by elected governors. The policy of allowing and even promoting local government by consent reached its highest form in the "commonwealth" model for local constitutional government that was adopted in the Philippines prior to their independence and that was subsequently adopted, in different and more limited forms, by Puerto Rico and the Northern Mariana Islands. Unfortunately, for residents of Puerto Rico and the other remaining U.S. territories, even the "commonwealth" model for local self-government has not resulted in equal citizenship rights or provided participation based on democratic consent in the federal government, whose laws remain the supreme authority under which they live.

The citizens of Puerto Rico have made important contributions to the political, economic, and social advancement of not only their own island, but of the United States generally. Their proud heritage as U.S. citizens reflects the spirit of America. Unfortunately, their cultural and economic assimilation into the United States has not been accompanied by equal citizenship under the U.S. Constitution. The residents of Puerto Rico are entitled to equality and full self-government at the level of national sovereignty, either as citizens of a coequal state of the Union or as citizens of an independent nation. Congress has the primary responsibility, under the Territorial Clause, to help put Puerto Rico on one of these paths toward self-governance. If Congress does not do so, the courts have a role they can play to protect the political and human rights of the residents of Puerto Rico—rights that are embodied in our nation's historic commitment against colonialism and that are recognized by the self-determination and decolonization provisions of the UN Charter, relevant UN General Assembly resolutions, the ICCPR, and other international covenants and commitments. If nothing else, the federal courts should address the discrepancy between the judicially determined legal and political policies that in large measure governed disposition of the territories of Hawaii and Alaska, on one hand, and of Puerto Rico, on the other.

Although the following discussion focuses on Puerto Rico, which is the largest and most heavily populated unincorporated territory, how the cutting-edge problems of less-than-equal citizenship and indefinite disenfranchisement are resolved for Puerto Rico will in all probability define the choices available to the other territories as well, given that they are being governed under the same unincorporated territory model.

AN ACTION PLAN FOR CONGRESS

The President's Task Force report has laid out an appropriate action plan for Congress.[3] It has urged Congress to agree upon the constitutionally viable paths toward a permanent nonterritorial status for Puerto Rico. In the task force's view, those options are limited to statehood and independence.[4] According to the task force, Congress should sponsor and recognize a self-determination process for Puerto Rico that would include a plebiscite in which the voters in Puerto Rico could express a preference between continuing Puerto Rico's current status as a territory and achieving one of the permanent nonterritorial statuses recognized by Congress.[5] If Puerto Rican voters elected to seek a permanent nonterritorial status, Congress would sponsor a second plebiscite that would ask the residents of Puerto Rico to choose between statehood and independence.[6]

History teaches us that Congress must take the initiative in framing the terms for resolution of Puerto Rico's political status. The simple truth is that the self-determination and status resolution processes in Puerto Rico are in a state of arrest. Congress should not wait for the residents of Puerto Rico (or the residents of other unincorporated territories) to petition Congress for a fully self-governing status, because only Congress can define and approve status options and the terms for status resolution. That responsibility and power derive from the Territorial Clause of the Constitution, which authorizes Congress to "dispose of and make all needful Rules and Regulations respecting the Territory . . . belonging to the United States,"[7] and from the Treaty of Peace with Spain, in which the United States agreed that Congress would determine the "civil rights and political status" of the inhabitants of Puerto Rico and other island territories acquired from Spain.[8] Furthermore, as the branch of government with primary responsibility over U.S. territories, Congress should take the initiative to ensure that the United States satisfies commitments made under international covenants, such as the ICCPR, to "promote the realization of the right of self-determination" and the rights of "universal and equal suffrage" for "all individuals within its territory and subject to its jurisdiction."[9]

Congress has the constitutional power and responsibility to define the political status options it is willing to recognize and to contrast those options with the unincorporated territory status that Puerto Rico has now. Unfortunately, for almost 100 years, Congress has used the reasoning of *Balzac* as an excuse for failing to exercise that power and responsibility. As a result, the record of Congress on political status resolution issues is one of disarray and weakness.[10] Congress should wait no longer to fulfill its constitutional responsibilities.

Local political status initiatives in Puerto Rico will be frustrated or will fail if Congress does not honestly define the constitutionally viable options for achieving full self-government. Historically, the only such options have been statehood (which has been most appropriate for territories for which admission to the Union has been socially, economically, and politically realistic), independence, or independent nationhood with a treaty of free association. Such a treaty was available in the case of those few island territories for which neither statehood nor full independence without a sustaining association was feasible.[11] Members of Congress (and certain political leaders in Puerto Rico) should stop pretending that some "enhanced commonwealth" status would avoid hard choices between statehood and independence. A "commonwealth" is simply a form of nonpermanent territorial status that implements limited local self-government at the discretion of Congress and leaves territorial residents subject to the unchecked power of a Congress in which they have no voting representatives. If this nonpermanent, local self-government option is to be presented as a political alternative to voters in Puerto Rico and other territories, it should be described honestly, for otherwise it could hardly be said that the voters' choice of commonwealth/territorial status represented informed consent of the governed.

It is time for the members of Congress to act with the same courage and principle that enabled 33 other territories to fulfill the promise of America in the years since 1789, by remembering that the founders of our nation staked their worldly fortunes and sacred honor on the moral necessity of equal citizenship and full government by consent of the governed. The President's Task Force has set out the appropriate plan of action to achieve that promise. Congress should follow it, or some version of it.

THE COURTS CAN PLAY A ROLE IF CONGRESS CONTINUES TO FALTER

As explained in detail previously, current territorial policy toward Puerto Rico and other unincorporated territories under U.S. control has created a political and legal subclass of citizens denied fundamental rights of national citizenship under the Constitution, as well as the right of self-determination provided by the ICCPR and other international accords recognized by the United States. Many of these problems can be traced back to the judicial interference of the Supreme Court on issues of territorial policy, as reflected in the Court's decisions in the *Insular Cases* and in *Balzac*. Although this author believes that Congress has the primary responsibility for redirecting U.S. territorial policy toward Puerto Rico and other U.S. territories, the courts can play a useful role by recognizing the errors in the Supreme Court's prior reasoning and by recommending that the Supreme Court overturn its decisions in the *Insular Cases* and in *Balzac*. By withdrawing federal judicial endorsement of those decisions, U.S. jurisprudence can be restored to the pre-*Balzac* anticolonial tradition of status resolution for U.S.-citizen populated territories, and the United States can conform to the international standards for self-determination and decolonization that it has recognized in more modern times.

If Congress does not fulfill its constitutional responsibilities, however, there may be an additional role the courts can play by affirming the human and political rights of territorial residents under well-recognized international accords and by calling upon the Congress to bring U.S. territorial policies into compliance with those accords.

Correcting the Supreme Court's Past Mistakes

By allowing Congress to govern U.S. citizens without extending equal rights under federal law, the Supreme Court's decisions in *Downes v. Bidwell*[12] and *Balzac* improperly created and legally institutionalized a subclass of people who were designated U.S. citizens for limited purposes of territorial rule, but denied the rights of U.S. citizens under the Constitution. If Congress does not reject this policy and practice, the courts should do so, affirming that there can be only one class of U.S. citizenship and that making a subclass of citizenship permanent or even indefinite is not a proper exercise of the power of Congress under the Territorial Clause and Naturalization Clause of the Constitution.

The subclass of less-than-equal citizenship created by *Balzac* imposed a condition and status on U.S. citizens in the unincorporated territories that is analogous to the subclass of freed slaves denied citizenship under the *Dred Scott* case of 1857[13] and that is legally and morally akin to the status of slaves under the infamous provision counting slaves as three-fifths of a person for apportionment of seats in the House of Representatives under Article I, Section 2, of the Constitution. It took the Civil War and Section 2 of the Fourteenth Amendment to repudiate the three-fifths compromise and the *Dred Scott* ruling, just as it took decades for the Supreme Court's decision in *Brown v. Board of Education*[14] to reverse its prior approval of separate-but-equal discrimination in *Plessy v. Ferguson*.[15] If given proper scrutiny now, it is doubtful that the rationale of *Balzac* could survive, just as the Court's rationales in the *Dred Scott* and *Plessy v. Ferguson* decisions did not survive subsequent review.[16] The courts should hesitate no longer in repudiating the unsustainable jurisprudence of *Balzac*, at least to the extent that it failed to make any distinction between the status of Puerto Rico when its residents were noncitizens and the status Puerto Rico acquired upon conferral of U.S. citizenship by Congress.

The recent reluctance of certain federal courts to deal with such issues because they ostensibly raise "political questions" ignores the fact that, by inventing the doctrine of "unincorporated territory" status out of whole cloth,[17] the Supreme Court improperly intruded deeply into a realm of territorial policy the Constitution assigned to the political branches of the government. By failing to follow precedents, such as *Rassmussen v. United States*,[18] which held that conferral of U.S. citizenship upon residents of a territory constituted a federal political status policy that established a higher order of "fundamental rights" under the Constitution than existed for noncitizens in the territories, the Supreme Court's decision in *Balzac* institutionalized second-class U.S. citizenship in Puerto Rico and encouraged Congress not to resolve the status of Puerto Rico in compliance with this nation's historical norms and international obligations. The political question doctrine ought not protect a line of improperly reasoned Supreme Court decisions that themselves represented an improper intrusion by the Court into political questions Congress should have resolved.

An example of this inconsistency in judicial reasoning can be found in the opinion of the U.S. District Judge in Puerto Rico who dismissed the most recent *Igartúa* case.[19] After acknowledging the unfairness of disenfranchising U.S. citizens who were serving as members of the U.S. military and after describing U.S. noncompliance at home with international self-determination standards as an "anomaly" that "has not gone unnoticed, neither by this nor other courts," the District Court's opinion argued that "in the various plebiscites to date the citizens of Puerto Rico have yet to resolve this anomaly themselves. Contrary to what some may passionately desire, it is not the function of this court to make future plebiscites irrelevant."[20] This interpretation of the court's duties is exactly contrary to how federal courts properly should frame the questions before them. For the reality is that self-determination in Puerto Rico, through a free and informed vote, may very well not take place until the courts untie the juridical knot of the *Balzac* doctrine. Judge Torruella recognized this reality in his dissent when *Igartúa* reached the U.S. Court of Appeals, in which he explained why it is inappropriate to pretend that status resolution for Puerto Rico is a purely political question, or that somehow the residents of the territory need merely to summon the political will to decide whether or not to seek independence or statehood.[21]

Thus, instead of invoking the political question doctrine, the courts need to restore the framework for territorial law that existed prior to *Balzac* and acknowledge that, under well-established separation of powers principles, territorial status questions must be decided by the political branches of government with due regard for the constitutional rights of citizens and not under judicial constructs like the unincorporated territory doctrine. The correction of past judicial mistakes will encourage Congress and the president to once again exercise their respective constitutional powers in a manner that accords with both American anticolonial traditions and international decolonization standards instituted in the modern era under the UN Charter.[22] Resolution of Puerto Rico's status will lead us beyond the warped jurisprudence of *Balzac* to a time when the United States has no unincorporated territories with indefinitely disenfranchised U.S. citizen populations who are denied access to a mechanism of self-determination and status resolution recognized under federal law.

Using Declaratory Relief to Affirm the Political and Human Rights of Territorial Residents

If the political branches of government do not step up and assume their constitutional responsibilities to resolve the political status of Puerto Rico, the courts can play an additional role by affirming that the residents of Puerto Rico and other U.S. territories have political and human rights that must no longer be ignored.

This author does not suggest that the courts make judicial determinations imposing a political status on Puerto Rico, nor does he suggest that the courts should resurrect the Northwest Ordinance model of territorial incorporation for Puerto Rico by judicial edict, for to do so would only repeat the Supreme Court's mistake in the *Insular Cases*. Instead, the courts should use their powers to issue declaratory relief to recognize that the "fundamental rights" principle expressed even in the *Balzac* ruling must include some procedure under federal law for democratic self-determination and status resolution.[23] It is within the authority and responsibility of the federal courts to determine the legal principles for reconciling our domestic and international standards of democracy and equality of citizenship rights with our practices as a nation at home and abroad.

If Congress fails to act soon, it may be appropriate to address several questions to the courts: Can the United States continue a federal territorial policy that denies U.S. citizens in an unincorporated territory the political or legal rights and processes that can end their disenfranchisement institutionalized under the U.S. constitutional system? Can residents of Puerto Rico indefinitely be denied access to a federally sponsored process of self-determination to resolve their status based on principles of government by consent of the governed and equal rights of national citizenship? Does U.S. citizenship confer political or legal rights beyond those of noncitizens? Is the U.S. commitment under Article 2 of the ICCPR[24]—to "promote the realization of the right of self-determination" for all individuals subject to its jurisdiction—a hollow pledge?

The federal courts can best answer these questions by declaring that all territorial residents have a right of access to a democratic self-determination process through which government by consent of the governed is at least possible. That right should be recognized as fundamental to U.S. citizenship and as a human right recognized by the United States under international law. The specific options for full self-government raise political questions, but the freedom to have a choice is a right no sovereign can deny to its citizens, especially not the United States of America. Anything less would suggest that the United States is maintaining a colonial policy toward Puerto Rico in violation of its commitments under the UN Charter and under General Assembly Resolution 748.[25]

If nothing else, the courts need to redeem the promise of America to all its citizens by ensuring that U.S. citizens in the territories have regular periodic opportunities to give their consent to continuation of territorial status. At a bare minimum, Congress should be compelled to afford that right to all U.S. citizens in the insular areas, and if it fails to do so, the courts should require it as a fundamental right of due process. Granting U.S. citizenship to Puerto Rico was made a consequence-free act by *Balzac*, and it is time for Congress or the courts to define some consequences in the form of democratic rights for our fellow citizens.

A self-determination process that would trigger votes on statehood or independence (including free association) only upon a majority vote to end territorial status would at least make some form of ultimate status resolution possible. Then if territorial status continued with consent of the governed, at least it would not be by operation of the current *Balzac*-based policy denying the fundamental right of self-determination.

Simply stated, Congress or the courts should offer Puerto Rico and the other U.S. territories a path to full and equal national citizenship under the U.S. Constitution, or through separate nationhood. For Puerto Rico and America, the time to decide has come.

Notes

[1] See discussion of the *Insular Cases* in the section beginning on page 46 of chapter 2.

[2] *Balzac v. Porto Rico*, 258 U.S. 298 (1922).

[3] President's Task Force on Puerto Rico's Status, *Report by the President's Task Force on Puerto Rico's Status* (December 2005), available at http://www.house.gov/fortuno/pdf/PuertoRicoBooklet.pdf. See discussion of the President's Task Force report in chapter 4.

[4] Ibid., 10. According to the President's Task Force, the independence alternative might be combined with a treaty-based compact of free association with the United States. Ibid., 8–9.

[5] Ibid., 10.

[6] Ibid.

[7] U.S. Constitution, art. 4, sec. 3, cl. 2.

[8] "Treaty of Peace between the United States of America and the Kingdom of Spain," April 11, 1899, *United States Statutes at Large* 30:1754.

[9] *International Covenant on Civil and Political Rights*, opened for signature December 16, 1966, 999 U.N.T.S. 171. See discussion of the ICCPR in the section beginning on page 61 of chapter 3.

[10] See, e.g., *United States–Puerto Rico Political Status Act*, HR 856, 105th Cong., 2d sess. (approved by the House of Representatives March 4, 1998); House Committee on Resources, *Report on United States–Puerto Rico Political Status Act*, prepared by Mr. Young of Alaska, 104th Cong., 2d sess., 1996, H. Rep. 104-713, Part 1; House Committee on Resources, *Report on United States–Puerto Rico Political Status Act*, prepared by Mr. Young of Alaska, 105th Cong., 1st sess., 1997, H. Rep. 105-131, Part 1; *Senate Resolution 279*, 105th Cong., 2d sess. (September 17, 1998); "Statement of Don Young and John T. Doolittle Regarding Non-Territorial Status Options for Puerto Rico," October 5, 2001, concerning Record of House Committee on Resources, *Puerto Rico–United States Bilateral Pact of Non-Territorial Permanent Union and Guaranteed Citizenship Act: Hearing on H.R. 4751*, 107th Cong., 1st sess., 2000, Committee Print 107-C.

[11] Other theoretical options include integration of a territory into an existing state or amendment of the Constitution to end the disenfranchisement of U.S. citizens who reside in territories.

[12] *Downes v. Bidwell*, 182 U.S. 244 (1901).

[13] *Scott v. Sandford*, 60 U.S. 393 (1857).

[14] *Brown v. Board of Education*, 347 U.S. 483 (1954).

[15] *Plessy v. Ferguson*, 163 U.S. 537 (1896).

[16] The federal statute excluding residents of Puerto Rico from overseas absentee voting (*U.S. Code* 42 (2006), § 1973ff–1973ff-6) is akin to many federal laws that discriminate against residents of Puerto Rico under the *Balzac* doctrine. See *Harris v. Rosario*, 446 U.S. 651 (1980).

[17] See *Downes v. Bidwell*, 182 U.S. 244 (1901); *Dorr v. United States*, 195 U.S. 138 (1904).

[18] *Rassmussen v. United States*, 197 U.S. 516 (1905).

[19] *Igartúa de la Rosa v. United States*, 331 F. Supp. 2d 76 (D.P.R. 2004).

[20] Ibid. at 81.

[21] *Igartúa de la Rosa v. United States*, 417 F.3d 145, 168 (1st Cir. 2005).

[22] "Charter of the United Nations and Statute of the International Court of Justice," June 26, 1945, ch. XI, *U.S. Statutes at Large* 59:1031 (signed at San Francisco June 26, 1945, ratified by the U.S. Senate July 28, 1945, approved by the president August 8, 1945, entered into force October 24, 1945).

[23] See section beginning on page 67 of chapter 3 for a discussion of the declaratory relief powers of U.S. courts.

[24] See the section beginning on page 61 of chapter 3 for a discussion of the ICCPR.

[25] See the section beginning on page 62 of chapter 3 for a discussion of General Assembly Resolution 748.

SELECT BIBLIOGRAPHY

Burnett, Christina Duffy. *United States: American Expansion and Territorial Deannexation*, 72 U. Chi. L. Rev. 797 (2005).

Burnett, Christina Duffy, and Burke Marshall, eds. *Foreign in a Domestic Sense: Puerto Rico, American Expansion, and the Constitution*. Durham, N.C.: Duke University Press, 2001.

Grupo de Investigadores Puertorriquenos. *Breakthrough from Colonialism: An Interdisciplinary Study of Statehood*. Río Piedras, Puerto Rico: Editorial de la Universidad de Puerto Rico, 1984.

Hills, Howard L. *Free Association for Micronesia and the Marshall Islands: A Transitional Political Status Model*, 27 Haw. L. Rev. 1 (2004).

______. *Compact of Free Association for Micronesia: Constitutional and International Law Issues*, 18 Int'l Law. 583 (1984).

Márquez, Carlos. "Independence: Could Puerto Rico Go It Alone?" *Caribbean Business* 34, no. 2 (January 19, 2006): 17–19 (Part 2 in a series of articles published by Carlos Márquez in January/February 2006 discussing Puerto Rico's political status and the President's Task Force report).

Odishelidze, Alexander, and Arthur Laffer. *Pay to the Order of Puerto Rico: The Cost of Dependence to the American Taxpayer*. Fairfax, Va.: Allegiance Press, 2004.

Perkins, Whitney T. *Denial of Empire: The United States and Its Dependencies*. Leyden, The Netherlands: A.W. Sythoff, 1962.

Pomeroy, Earl S. *The Territories and the United States, 1861–1890: Studies in Colonial Administration*. Philadelphia: University of Pennsylvania Press, 1947.

President's Task Force on Puerto Rico's Status. *Report by the President's Task Force on Puerto Rico's Status* (December 2005), available at http://www.house.gov/fortuno/pdf/PuertoRicoBooklet.pdf.

Rosselló, Pedro. *The Unfinished Business of American Democracy*. San Juan, Puerto Rico: Public Policy Institute of the Ana G. Méndez University System, 2005.

Sparrow, Bartholomew H. *The Insular Cases and the Emergence of American Empire*. Lawrence: University Press of Kansas, 2006.

Thornburgh, Dick. "Dred Scott and Balzac—A Legacy of Equality Denied." *San Juan Star*, July 14, 2004.

INDEX

Page numbers followed by the letter *n* refer to notes.

ABOUT THE AUTHOR

Dick Thornburgh is a former attorney general of the United States, a former governor of the Commonwealth of Pennsylvania, and a former undersecretary general of the United Nations. Since January 1, 1994, Mr. Thornburgh has been counsel to Kirkpatrick & Lockhart Preston Gates Ellis LLP in Washington, D.C.

During his many years as a public official and as a private citizen, Mr. Thornburgh has frequently addressed the political and legal rights of U.S. citizens who reside in Puerto Rico. As a result of his experiences at the United Nations and as a frequent participant in international efforts to encourage and protect democratic institutions, the rule of law, and the rights of voters, he is well aware of this nation's international commitments to democracy and self-determination. Mr. Thornburgh has frequently written, spoken, and testified before Congress on these subjects.

This work is based, in part, on research that Mr. Thornburgh did as attorney general in preparation for his testimony in 1991 before the U.S. Senate Committee on Energy and Natural Resources, which was considering the political status of Puerto Rico, and in connection with the brief he submitted in 2005, as *amicus curiae,* to the U.S. Court of Appeals for the First Circuit, in a case concerning voting rights in Puerto Rico. Mr. Thornburgh has also been an adviser to nonprofit educational foundations dedicated to promoting informed self-determination for the people of Puerto Rico and to understanding the application of U.S. law and policy to Puerto Rico.